HSE
Health & Safety
Executive

A guide to the Gas Safety (Management) Regulations 1996

GUIDANCE ON REGULATIONS

HSE BOOKS

This guidance, which is issued by the Health and
Safety Executive, explains what the Executive will
expect to see included in safety cases submitted to
it for acceptance under the Gas Safety
(Management) Regulations 1996. It also gives
practical guidance on the requirements of the
Regulations and, while following it is not
compulsory, if you do follow it you will normally
be doing enough to comply with these
requirements. Health and safety inspectors seek to
secure compliance with the law and may refer to
this guidance as illustrating good practice.

Contents

Regulation 1   Citation and commencement   *1*

Regulation 2   Interpretation   *1*

Regulation 3   Duties on persons conveying gas   *6*

Regulation 4   Revision of safety cases   *7*

Regulation 5   Duty to conform with safety case   *8*

Regulation 6   Co-operation   *8*

Regulation 7   Gas escapes and investigations   *11*

Regulation 8   Content and other characteristics of gas   *17*

Regulation 9   Keeping of documents   *18*

Regulation 10   Transitional provisions   *19*

Regulation 11   Exemptions   *20*

Regulation 12   Repeals, revocations and amendment   *20*

Content of safety cases: general guidance   *22*

Schedule 1   Particulars to be included in safety case of a person conveying gas   *25*

Schedule 2   Particulars to be included in safety case of a network emergency co-ordinator   *41*

Schedule 3   Content and other characteristics of gas   *46*

Citation and commencement

These Regulations may be cited as the Gas Safety (Management) Regulations 1996 and shall come into force on 1st April 1996 except regulation 8 which shall come into force on 31st October 1996.

Interpretation

(1)   In these Regulations, unless the context otherwise requires -

"the 1994 Regulations" means the Gas Safety (Installation and Use) Regulations 1994[(a)];

"distribution main" has the same meaning as in regulation 2(1) of the 1994 Regulations;

"electricity generating station" includes an electricity generating station used for generating electricity for use on the same premises on which it is situated;

(a) SI 1994/1886 amended by SI 1996/550.

1   An electricity generating station refers to those facilities which supply electricity to:

(a)   the national grid; or

(b)   the premises on which they are situated; or

(c)   both.

This definition also includes combined heat and power units.

"emergency control" has the same meaning as in regulation 2(1) of the 1994 Regulations;

2   An emergency control is a valve intended for use by the consumer for turning off the gas supply in an emergency. An emergency control will always be found at the end of the service pipe but additional controls may be found in premises, for example, if the primary meter is moved to assist a disabled person.

"emergency service provider" means a person appointed pursuant to regulation 7(11);

"the Executive" means the Health and Safety Executive;

"gas" means any substance in a gaseous state which consists wholly or mainly of methane;

3   These Regulations are intended to cover the transport of natural gas to the public. They do not cover gases such as liquefied petroleum gas (LPG), coke-oven gases, etc.

"gas fittings" means gas fittings as defined in regulation 2(1) of the 1994 Regulations as if the phrase "(other than the purpose of an industrial process carried out on industrial premises)" did not appear in that definition;

Regulation

Section 2(1)

Regulation

Regulation 2(1)

4   Gas fittings are any pipes, meters, appliances etc on the consumer's side of the emergency control at the end of the service pipe. The definition applies to gas fittings at domestic, commercial and industrial premises.

"gas processing facility" means any gas processing facility which -

   (a)   blends or purifies gas, removes from gas any of its constituent gases or separates from gas any oil or water; and

   (b)   is situated at a terminal which receives gas directly or indirectly from a gas production facility;

5   A gas processing facility is the terminal which first receives gas from a gas production facility but does not include, for example, a BG TransCo reception terminal.

"gas production facility" means a facility for the extraction of gas from strata or for the manufacture of gas;

6   Both onshore and offshore facilities provide gas to 'gas processing facilities'. This may be direct from the production facility or indirectly, for example, via an offshore gas gathering system.

"installation pipework" has the same meaning as in regulation 2(1) of the 1994 Regulations;

"interconnector" means a pipeline used for the conveyance of gas to Great Britain from another country;

"network" shall be construed in accordance with paragraphs (2) to (4);

"network emergency co-ordinator" shall be construed in accordance with paragraphs (2) and (3) of regulation 3;

"pipe" includes a pipeline, distribution main, service pipe and any ancillary plant connected to a pipe and used for the conveyance of gas, but it does not include a pipe downstream of an emergency control;

7   For the purposes of these Regulations, the definition of the word 'pipe' does not include any pipe on the consumer's side of the emergency control at the end of the service pipe.

"safety case" shall be construed in accordance with paragraph (5);

"service pipe" has the same meaning as in regulation 2(1) of the 1994 Regulations;

8   A service pipe connects the distribution main to individual premises, terminating at the outlet of the emergency control immediately upstream of installation pipework and other gas fittings.

"supply emergency" means an emergency endangering persons and arising from a loss of pressure in a network or any part thereof.

9   The loss of pressure referred to in the Regulations would usually be caused by insufficient gas being present in the network, ie demand exceeding supply. This could be caused by a failure on the supply side due to an incident offshore, at a terminal, or on a main transmission pipe. It could also be caused by an incorrect forecast for short-term gas consumption. In some circumstances, an accidental gas leak from the network could give rise to a

2

significant or total loss of pressure as a consequence of the leak, or the actions of the emergency services executing their duties under regulation 7.

(2)   Any reference in these Regulations to a network is, subject to paragraphs (3) and (4), a reference to a connected network of pipes used for the conveyance of gas from a gas processing facility, a storage facility or an interconnector, except a connected network of pipes used exclusively for conveying gas to non-domestic premises.

10   A network starts from a gas processing facility, storage facility or interconnector importing gas into Great Britain but does not include it. However, where a pipeline, for the time being, is used to convey gas from Great Britain, it will be necessary for the gas transporter (see paragraph 16) on that pipeline to prepare a safety case in accordance with these Regulations. The end of the network is the outlet of the emergency control at the end of the service pipe (see Figure 1 for a schematic diagram of the network).

11   These Regulations do not apply to stand alone networks which only convey gas to industrial and other non-domestic premises, eg factories, warehouses or office blocks. Thus, for example, a dedicated pipeline or distribution system conveying gas only to non-domestic premises from a gas processing facility would not be a network within the meaning of these Regulations. Those who convey gas on such a system would not, therefore, be required to produce a safety case, or otherwise comply with these Regulations.

12   Such stand alone networks are different from those networks of pipes which may be used to convey gas both to domestic and non-domestic premises. Thus, a system of pipes which may only be being used to convey gas to non-domestic premises would be subject to the Regulations if it was, itself, connected directly or indirectly to pipes operated by another transporter(s) conveying gas to domestic premises.

(3)   A network does not include pipes upstream from a junction on a pipe used exclusively for conveying gas to an electricity generating station; and in this paragraph the reference to a junction on a pipe used exclusively for conveying gas to an electricity generating station is a reference to the point where the upstream end of the pipe joins a pipe used for another purpose.

13   This regulation applies to those pipes used exclusively for conveying gas complying with Part I of Schedule 3 to electricity generating stations and where, somewhere along its length, a pipe which is part of a network within the meaning of these Regulations joins it. The pipe downstream of the join, ie between the join and the power station, will form part of the network and a safety case will be required for that section of pipe.

(4)   Where gas which does not conform with the requirements referred to in regulation 8(1) is conveyed from a gas processing facility for treatment or blending so as to bring it into conformity with those requirements, any pipes used exclusively for conveying gas from that facility to the point where the gas is treated or blended or to non-domestic premises or to both, shall not be treated as part of a network for the purposes of these Regulations.

14   Pipes which are used to convey out-of-specification gas to a treatment or blending point, or to non-domestic premises, or both, are not part of the network and will not require a safety case. A treatment point is the point where out-of-specification gas is brought within the specification of Part I of Schedule 3 before it enters the network. A blending point is the point where out-of-specification gas is mixed with other gas on the network to produce gas of a new composition which is within the specification set out in Part I of Schedule 3.

Figure 1 The network

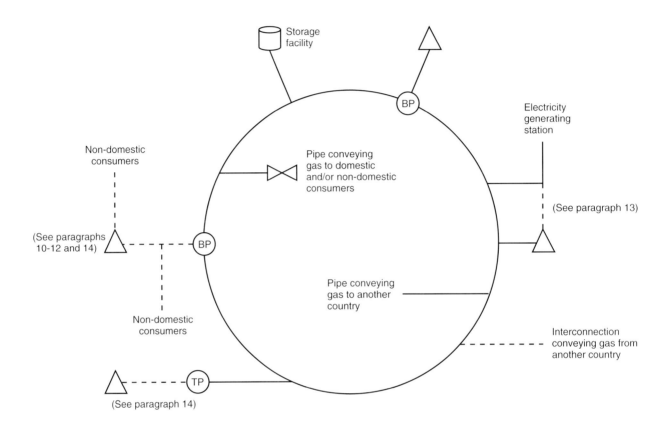

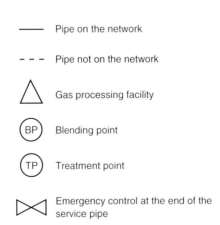

These represent the two ways by which out-of-specification gas can be conveyed through pipes and processed prior to introduction into the network. However, when gas which conforms to Part I of Schedule 3 is conveyed periodically through the same pipes, these pipes will form part of the network. Safety cases will need to address both situations.

(5) Any reference in these Regulations to a safety case is a reference to a document containing the particulars required by the provision of these Regulations pursuant to which the safety case is prepared, and -

(a) insofar as the document contains other particulars it shall not be treated as part of the safety case for the purposes of these Regulations;

(b) nothing in these Regulations shall require the particulars to relate to a source of risk other than the gas itself.

15 A safety case for a gas transporter needs to conform to the requirements of Schedule 1 to the Regulations. A safety case for the network emergency co-ordinator (NEC) needs to address the requirements laid down in Schedule 2 to these Regulations. The safety case should cover the relevant issues concerning only the safe conveyance of gas.

16 Throughout this guidance, the terminology used is, as far as possible, consistent with that used in the Gas Act 1986 as amended by the Gas Act 1995. Thus, the terms 'supplier' and 'shipper' have the same meaning as section 7A(1) and 7A(2) to the Act. The guidance also refers to 'gas transporters'. These are those people who either hold a 'public gas transporter' (PGT) licence, or who physically convey gas through pipes but are exempt from the need to hold a PGT licence.

(6) Any reference in these Regulations to the Executive accepting a safety case or revision thereof is a reference to the Executive notifying in writing the person who prepared it that it is satisfied with the case for health and safety made out in it.

17 A safety case, or a revised safety case, has not been accepted by the Health and Safety Executive (HSE) until the person preparing it has been notified of that fact in writing.

(7) Any reference in these Regulations to the conveyance of gas is a reference to the conveyance of gas through pipes.

18 Conveyance of gas by means other than pipes is not covered by, nor is relevant to, these Regulations.

(8) Any reference in these Regulations to conveying gas in a network includes a reference to conveying gas in any part of the network.

19 All parts of a network (see paragraphs 10-13) are covered by the Regulations.

(9) Any reference in these Regulations to preventing a supply emergency is a reference to preventing a supply emergency from occurring or continuing.

20 One of the principal aims of these Regulations is to minimise the risk of a supply emergency occurring, or if that is not possible, to minimise its duration.

(10) In these Regulations any reference, in relation to a network, to the network emergency co-ordinator is a reference to the network emergency co-ordinator who has prepared and had accepted a safety case relating to that network pursuant to regulation 3(2) or 10(4).

(11) Any reference in these Regulations to a person supplying or conveying gas, preparing a safety case or carrying out work in relation to a gas fitting is a reference to a person who does so in the course of a business or other undertaking carried on by him.

21   Businesses or undertakings are covered by the Regulations whether they are carried out for profit or not; for example charities, institutions and other operations run on a voluntary basis are included.

(12) Unless the context otherwise requires, any reference in these Regulations to -

(a)   a numbered regulation or Schedule is a reference to the regulation or Schedule in these Regulations so numbered;

(b)   a numbered paragraph is a reference to the paragraph so numbered in the regulation or Schedule in which the reference appears.

Duties on persons conveying gas

(1)   No person shall convey gas in a network unless -

(a)   he has prepared a safety case containing the particulars specified in Schedule 1 and that safety case has been accepted by the Executive; and

(b)   where any other person is conveying gas in that network, there is a sole network emergency co-ordinator for the network.

22   All gas transporters must prepare a safety case, submit it to HSE and have it accepted before beginning operations (but see transitional arrangements, under regulation 10, for gas transporters operating on a network before 1 April 1997). Where two or more gas transporters are operating on a network, there should also be a sole network emergency co-ordinator (NEC) for that network whose safety case has been accepted by HSE.

(2)   For the purposes of these Regulations a network emergency co-ordinator is, subject to paragraph (3), a person who has prepared a safety case containing the particulars specified in Schedule 2 and has had that safety case accepted by the Executive.

23   The NEC does not come into existence, in a legal sense, until his safety case has been prepared, submitted and accepted by HSE.

(3)   Where a network emergency co-ordinator has given written notice to the Executive and to all persons conveying gas in the network that he no longer intends to act in that capacity, he shall not be the network emergency co-ordinator for the purposes of these Regulations from the time such notice takes effect (which shall not be less than 6 months after it was given).

24   An NEC can relinquish his role by giving at least 6 months notice. The 6-month notice period is designed to allow gas transporters on the network to agree a replacement NEC, and for that successor to prepare, submit and have a safety case accepted by HSE.

(4)   Nothing in these Regulations shall prevent a person who conveys gas in a network from also being the network emergency co-ordinator.

25   An NEC can come from the same organisation as one of the gas transporters forming part of the network. The gas conveyance part of the organisation would, however, need to submit to the control of the NEC in the event of a supply emergency.

Revision of safety cases

(1) A person who has prepared a safety case pursuant to these Regulations shall revise its contents whenever it is appropriate, but nothing in this paragraph shall require him to have the revision accepted by the Executive.

(2) Where a revision proposed to be made under paragraph (1) will render the safety case materially different from the last version accepted by the Executive pursuant to these Regulations, the revision shall not be made unless the Executive has accepted the revision, and for the purposes of this paragraph in determining whether a proposed revision will render the safety case materially different from the version referred to above, regard shall be had to the cumulative effect of that proposed revision and any previous revisions made under paragraph (1) but not subject to this paragraph.

26   The safety case is a living document and should be kept up to date to take account of, for example, alterations to the gas transporter's system, changes to the method of operation, management structure etc. Even apparently minor changes should be assessed and arrangements made for logging them and ensuring all relevant documentation is updated as appropriate, including copies of such documents that may be in use. Apart from the obvious operational need to keep the safety case up to date, systematic logging of modifications will help gas transporters to demonstrate to HSE that they are continuing to operate, as required by regulation 5, in conformity with their safety case.

27   Where proposed modifications have a material effect on the safety case, the safety case, or relevant parts of it, should be resubmitted to HSE for acceptance. Such changes should not be implemented until the new safety case (or parts) has been accepted by HSE; but see also paragraph 32.

28   Whether a change is material will often depend on how much more gas is likely to be conveyed as a result of any new development, in comparison with the overall size of the gas transporter's system. Thus a new supply to a housing estate may not constitute a material change to a large gas transporter, but might to a smaller one. Alternatively, the need for a material change may become apparent following an accident, or 'near miss', or as a result of advances in technology.

29   To enable a broad understanding to be developed in advance with HSE on the types of change that could be regarded as material, duty holders will no doubt wish to liaise closely with HSE during the preparation of their safety case, and to propose relevant criteria for determining what is material in their safety case. In addition to pipeline infrastructure changes, changes in policies, eg security of supply criteria, procedures, use of storage gas by the transporter for daily balancing or other operational reasons, computer and communication systems and key personnel could all have a material effect on the arrangements described in the safety case. Minor changes in day-to-day management need not be submitted, but changes of operator or ownership, the contracting out of or change to key safety functions, eg emergency service provision, are examples of changes which could merit the submission of a revised safety case or part of it. The cumulative effect of a series of minor changes might also require resubmission of a safety case. Any change should therefore be viewed in the context of its impact on the safety case which has been accepted by HSE. It is important to emphasise that it is the gas transporter's responsibility, in the light of all the circumstances and the criteria agreed with HSE, to determine what constitutes a material change. In cases of doubt advice may be sought from HSE.

(3) A person who has prepared a safety case which has been accepted by the Executive pursuant to these Regulations shall make a thorough review of its contents at least every three years.

30 Safety cases should in any event be reviewed every three years and a report sent to HSE, as required under regulation 9(1)(e). The main purpose of the review is to ensure that gas transporters re-examine the entire contents of the safety case at regular intervals. The report submitted should reflect the fact that a review has been carried out and indicate the conclusions reached. In particular, it should include what, if any, changes to the safety case have been identified as being necessary as a result of the review. If a material change is considered necessary, the revised safety case should be submitted to HSE for acceptance.

Regulation 5

Duty to conform with safety case

(1) Where a person has prepared and has had accepted a safety case pursuant to these Regulations he shall ensure, so long as he conveys gas in the network to which the safety case relates or remains a network emergency co-ordinator, as the case may be, that the procedures and arrangements described in the safety case and any revision thereof are followed.

31 After a safety case has been accepted by HSE, arrangements will need to be put in place to ensure the safety case is being followed, including any revisions made under regulation 4. An audit review, or other appropriate mechanism to check on compliance, will be necessary (see paragraph 6 of Schedule 1 and paragraph 4 of Schedule 2 to these Regulations).

(2) In criminal proceedings for a contravention of paragraph (1) it shall be a defence for the accused to prove that -

(a) in the particular circumstances of the case it was not in the best interests of health and safety to follow the procedures or arrangements concerned and there was insufficient time to revise the safety case pursuant to regulation 4; or

(b) the commission of the offence was due to a contravention by another person of regulation 6 and the accused had taken all reasonable precautions and exercised all due diligence to ensure that the procedures or arrangements were followed.

32 Regulation 5(2)(a) relates to situations where compliance with the safety case might lead to a greater risk to safety than if it was breached, eg changes needed in an emergency situation not foreseen in the original safety case. Regulation 5(2)(b) relates to situations where, although the safety case has not been complied with, this was caused by an error, omission or criminal act by some other person, especially those listed in regulation 6(2). Thus, for example, if it could be shown that a supply emergency was caused by the negligent actions of a gas shipper or terminal operator, then no blame would attach to the gas transporter if he had done everything it was reasonable for someone in his position to do given all the circumstances.

Regulation 6

Co-operation

(1) Every person to whom this paragraph applies shall co-operate so far as is necessary with a person conveying gas in a network and with a network emergency co-ordinator to enable them to comply with the provisions of these Regulations.

(2)   Paragraph (1) applies to -

(a)   a person conveying gas in the network;

(b)   an emergency service provider;

(c)   the network emergency co-ordinator in relation to a person conveying gas;

(d)   a person conveying gas in pipes which are not part of a network by virtue of regulation 2(3) or (4);

(e)   the holder of a licence issued under section 7A of the Gas Act 1986[(a)];

(f)   a person exempted under section 6A(1) of the Gas Act 1986[(b)] from paragraph (b) or (c) of section 5(1) of that Act;

(g)   a person referred to in paragraph 5(1) of Schedule 2A to the Gas Act 1986;

(h)   the person in control of a gas production facility, a gas processing facility, a storage facility or an interconnector supplying gas to the network.

(a) 1986 c.44; section 7A was inserted by section 6 of the Gas Act 1995.
(b) Section 6A of the Gas Act 1986 was inserted by section 4 of the Gas Act 1995.

33   This regulation creates a duty on those cited in regulation 6(2) to co-operate with gas transporters and the NEC as far as is necessary to enable them to comply with these Regulations. For a network to operate safely and to minimise the risk of a supply emergency, it is necessary for gas transporters to have appropriate information about the supply and demand of gas on their part of the network, so that the network as a whole remains in balance. The practical arrangements to achieve this will be set out in the transporter's safety case, including arrangements and operational procedures which the gas transporter has agreed with other duty holders (see paragraph 80).

34   Other situations where co-operation will be important include when a gas escape occurs or where an incident notifiable under regulation 6(1) of the Reporting of Injuries, Diseases and Dangerous Occurrences Regulations 1995 (RIDDOR) has occurred. This will involve the exchange of information and co-ordination of action to deal with both the incident itself and to complete the necessary investigation (see regulation 7 of these Regulations).

(3)   The reference in paragraph (2)(h) to the person in control of a production facility is -

(a)   where the facility is a fixed installation within the meaning of regulation 2(1) of the Offshore Installations and Pipeline Works (Management and Administration) Regulations 1995[(c)], an operator within the meaning of that regulation;

(b)   where the facility is a borehole site within the meaning of regulation 2(1) of the Borehole Sites and Operations Regulations 1995[(d)], an operator within the meaning of that regulation.

(4)   A person conveying gas in a network may, subject to paragraph (5), direct a person not to consume gas for the period specified in the direction.

(c) SI 1995/738.
(d) SI 1995/2038.

(5)   A direction under paragraph (4) may -

(a)   only be given where it is necessary to prevent a supply emergency or to prevent danger arising from the use of gas not conforming with the requirements of regulation 8;

(b)   be given orally or in writing and may be withdrawn at any time.

35   This regulation provides for gas transporters to instruct consumers to cease using gas where it is necessary to avoid a supply emergency developing, or if one develops to minimise its impact, or to prevent danger arising from the use of gas not conforming with the requirements of regulation 8.

36   Depending on the circumstances, eg the number of people involved or the speed with which a supply emergency develops, the transporter may make the direction orally, for example by telephone, or by fax, or otherwise in writing. The main risks associated with a supply emergency arise from the partial or total shutdown of the network. In these circumstances it will be necessary for individual consumers to cease using gas safely, to make the pipeline and distribution mains safe and subsequently to reinstate the gas supply safely. In essence, if pressure has been lost in a gas main, all the affected pipework needs to be brought to atmospheric pressure, then purged of residual gas, before being repressurised and brought back on stream. Any premises downstream of the point where pressure was lost would have to be entered to purge any air, or other contaminant which may have entered the system when gas pressure was lost, and for the appliances to be relit.

37   It follows that the fewer premises involved, the lower the risk. If the situation allows, it will normally be preferable for a few large industrial consumers to stop using gas, rather than many domestic consumers or other low volume consumers. It might also be appropriate for gas transporters to make appeals to domestic and other low volume consumers to reduce consumption.

38   In some cases, it may be appropriate for the supplier to assist the gas transporter in managing the emergency. However, it will be essential that all consumers understand that the supplier is operating under the directions of the transporter and that consumers are aware of the need to follow any directions issued by the gas transporter.

(6)   Where a direction is given to a person pursuant to paragraph (4), that person shall comply with it during the period specified in the direction except that this shall not require him to comply with a direction after it has been withdrawn.

39   Where the gas transporter has issued an instruction to a consumer to cease using gas, the consumer must by law follow that direction. However, it will be important for gas transporters to satisfy themselves that consumers are in a position to comply with any direction issued, ie there is sufficient lead time for consumers to cease using gas in a safe manner.

(7)   In criminal proceedings for a contravention of paragraph (6) it shall be a defence for the accused to prove that he had no knowledge of the direction.

(8)   A person who conveys gas in a network shall, where he is requested to do so by a person proposing to carry out work in relation to a gas fitting, provide him with information about the operating pressures of the gas at the outlet of a service pipe.

Gas escapes and investigations

(1)   It shall be the duty of British Gas p.l.c. to provide a continuously manned telephone service (which shall be contactable within Great Britain by the use of one telephone number) for enabling persons to report an escape of gas from a network or from a gas fitting supplied with gas from a network.

40   British Gas (BG) plc will provide a continuously staffed national 0800 freephone number for use by the public, consumers and the emergency services in the event of a gas escape (gas escapes include actual or suspected emission of carbon monoxide (CO) from gas appliances), or a fire or explosion where gas is suspected to have been involved. Gas escapes can occur at any time and there should be sufficient trained and competent personnel to ensure that all calls are answered promptly whatever the time of day or night. In order to avoid delays in relaying information to the emergency service provider, BG telephone operators will need an outline script which will enable them to:

(a)   establish the precise location of the emergency;

(b)   establish whether the leak is controllable (ie on the consumer's side of the emergency control adjacent to the meter) or uncontrollable (ie on the transporter's side);

(c)   advise callers how to turn off the gas at the emergency control, and confirm that this has been done; except where the emergency control is in a cellar or other confined space, where there is also a smell of gas, when the advice should be not to enter but vacate the premises;

(d)   advise callers to open doors and windows to ventilate the property and warn them against operating any electrical appliances, in any way. They should also be advised not to smoke and to avoid using anything that could be a possible source of ignition;

(e)   establish whether there are fumes (escape of CO into the room), and if it is possible to identify the appliance; and

(f)   advise callers where an escape of CO is suspected of the immediate steps to be taken, namely to turn off all appliances which may be emitting CO and not to use them until they have been checked by the emergency service provider.

(2)   Where British Gas p.l.c. is notified of such an escape of gas it shall, if it is not responsible for preventing the escape under paragraphs (4) or (5), report it forthwith to the person who is.

41   BG plc is required to contact the relevant gas transporter, or their emergency service provider (where different), immediately when an emergency arises from a gas escape or suspected emission of CO. BG plc needs to prepare and maintain efficient methods of collecting and recording up-to-date information on the geographical areas covered by each gas transporter and/or emergency service provider. It will also need to establish arrangements to demonstrate that notifications are passed on promptly. It is possible that calls relating to LPG may be reported to BG plc. Although these Regulations do not apply to LPG, liquefied petroleum gas suppliers have duties under other Regulations to provide an emergency response. BG plc may want to give consideration to the arrangements it has with the appropriate organisation or its emergency service provider for dealing with such misdirected calls.

(3)   A person referred to in regulation 6(2)(a) to (c) and the holder of a licence issued under section 7A(1) of the Gas Act 1986 who discovers or is notified of any such escape of gas (other than by virtue of a report made to him pursuant to paragraph (2)) shall report it forthwith to British Gas p.l.c.

42   On some occasions consumers may contact suppliers, gas transporters or emergency service providers directly, rather than the 0800 number. Suppliers, gas transporters and emergency service providers will need to be able to demonstrate that they have adequate arrangements for dealing with misdirected calls. They should agree procedures with BG plc for the recording and passing on of information, for example, training staff, and the provision of a script which will enable them to obtain the same information as BG plc telephone operators (see paragraph 40). During out-of-office hours it might be more appropriate for suppliers to establish phone call diversion facilities. In order to comply with their duties under regulation 7(4) and (5) gas transporters, or the emergency service provider, notified through a misdirected call from the public of an emergency in their area of responsibility, should respond to that emergency without waiting for renotification from BG plc. However, they will still need to notify the emergency to BG plc.

(4)   Where any gas escapes from a network the person conveying the gas in the part of the network from which the gas escapes shall, as soon as is reasonably practicable after being so informed of the escape, attend the place where the gas is escaping, and within 12 hours of being so informed of the escape, he shall prevent the gas escaping.

(5)   Where any gas escapes from a gas fitting supplied with gas from a network, the person conveying the gas in the part of the network immediately upstream of the emergency control for the supply of gas to that fitting shall, as soon as is reasonably practicable after being so informed of the escape, attend the place where the gas is escaping, and within 12 hours of being so informed of the escape, he shall prevent the gas escaping.

43   Gas transporters/emergency service providers should attend the emergency, as soon as reasonably practicable, after receiving a report of a gas escape. They will also need to make arrangements to ensure that reports of emergencies can be received and responded to 24 hours a day. Once at the emergency, appropriate steps should be taken to bring the situation under control, and to make the situation safe as quickly as possible. The 12-hour period contained in the regulation is the maximum time that should normally be taken to stop gas escaping (see also paragraph 47).

44   Gas transporters/emergency service providers will need to ensure that:

(a)   where appropriate they are registered with CORGI, ie for work on gas fittings and installation pipework;

(b)   they employ competent operatives with sufficient knowledge, appropriate equipment, practical skill and experience to deal with all foreseeable emergency situations. The Health and Safety Commission Approved Code of Practice *Standards of training in safe gas installation* (ISBN 0 11 883966 7), for example, provides practical guidance on standards of training in safe gas installation;

(c)   sufficient numbers of operatives are available to deal promptly with each emergency no matter how large;

(d)   sufficient numbers of operatives, with appropriate rights-of-entry powers, are available to make situations safe where, for example, gas may have escaped into vacant property; and

(e)   they establish written procedures for operatives to follow.

45   The primary duty on gas transporters/emergency service providers in the event of an emergency is to make the situation safe. They will need to:

(a)   establish the cause of the escape and take action to make the situation safe by preventing gas from escaping; and/or

(b)   respond to reports of suspected or actual escapes of CO and make the situation safe.

46   If the reported gas escape is from a distribution main, consumers may suffer a loss of pressure, a total loss of gas supply, or both, while the leak is being repaired. Operatives attending such emergencies need to be prepared, fully trained and competent to ensure safe disconnection of the gas supply, and safe reinstatement including checking all appliances for obvious visible signs of spillage of products of combustion when appliances are relit.

47   If gas transporters/emergency service providers find an appliance which is spilling products of combustion, whether in response to a report of a suspected escape of CO, or when relighting appliances after a loss of supply, they should tell the consumer that further use of the appliance unless and until it is repaired is an offence, and seek to persuade the consumer to allow them to disconnect it. Gas transporters/emergency service providers have an obligation under regulation 7(5) to prevent the escape of gas. Therefore, if the consumer refuses to allow the appliance to be disconnected, the gas transporter (or emergency service provider) should exercise his rights-of-entry powers to deal with dangerous appliances. In such circumstances it would be appropriate to use these powers physically to disconnect the individual appliance from the installation pipework. Any appliance which is judged to be dangerous should be suitably labelled to this effect. A report on certain dangerous appliances must be made to HSE (as required under regulation 6(2) of RIDDOR). In the case of rented property the gas transporter/emergency service provider should inform both the tenant and the landlord (or their managing agent) that an appliance is considered dangerous and explain the appropriate action to be taken.

48   Where gas leaks are reported in factories, gas transporters/emergency service providers will need to consider the possible dangers of simply disconnecting the gas supply. There may be processes which depend on the gas directly or indirectly which, if terminated in an uncontrolled way, might have serious safety consequences. It would be sensible for leaks in factory premises to be dealt with only in consultation with the occupier who will be able to provide advice on any related safety consequences. The arrangements to cover all the circumstances described in paragraphs 43-48 will need to be set out in the gas transporter's safety case.

(6)   Where a person conveying gas in a network has reasonable cause to suspect that gas conveyed by him which has escaped has entered, or may enter, any premises, he shall, so far as is reasonably practicable, take all the steps necessary to avert danger to persons from such entry.

49   If gas transporters suspect that gas has escaped from part of their network into any premises, including open countryside which is part of agricultural premises, they should ensure, so far as is reasonably practicable, that people are not endangered by the escape. This may involve alerting the occupiers of the premises, advising them to open windows and doors, arranging for the evacuation of premises and, if necessary, using rights-of-entry powers to enter unoccupied premises to make the situation safe.

(7)   If the responsible person for any premises knows or has reason to suspect that gas is escaping from a gas fitting in those premises supplied with gas from a network he shall immediately take all reasonable steps to cause the supply of gas to be shut off at such place as may be necessary to prevent further escape of gas.

(8)   If gas continues to escape into those premises after the supply of gas has been shut off or when a smell of gas persists, the responsible person for the premises discovering such escape or smell shall immediately give notice of the escape or smell to British Gas p.l.c.

50   Where a gas escape is suspected or known to be occurring, the responsible person (see paragraph 64) should close the emergency control which is usually adjacent to the meter. If the smell of gas persists, the responsible person should immediately notify BG plc that there is a suspected leak of gas. In the case of suspected escape of CO the responsible person should turn off any appliances he suspects are emitting CO and contact BG plc immediately. However, if the responsible person is confident that a particular appliance is the source of the escape, he should ensure the appliance is not used and contact a CORGI registered installer to repair, replace, or otherwise make safe that appliance.

(9)   Where an escape of gas has been stopped by shutting off the supply, no person shall cause or permit the supply to be reopened (other than in the course of repair) until all necessary steps have been taken to prevent a recurrence of such escape.

(10)   In any proceedings against a person for an offence consisting of a contravention of paragraphs (4) or (5) above it shall, in so far as the contravention is not preventing the escape of gas within the period of 12 hours referred to in those paragraphs, be a defence for the person to prove that it was not reasonably practicable for him effectually to prevent the gas from escaping within that period, and that he did effectually prevent the escape of gas as soon as it was reasonably practicable for him to do so.

51   There may be circumstances, eg a severe fracture of a mains pipe, when it will not be feasible to repair the pipe within 12 hours. Gas transporters will, however, need to ensure that the situation is brought under control and made safe within 12 hours in order to meet the requirements of this regulation. Where it is not possible to prevent the leak within 12 hours, gas transporters/emergency service providers will need to demonstrate that they took all reasonably practicable steps to do so.

(11)   A person conveying gas may appoint another person to act on his behalf to prevent an escape of gas, and where he does so in advance of discovering or being notified of such an escape -

(a)   he shall notify British Gas p.l.c. of the name of the person appointed;

(b)   the appointee shall in relation to the escape be responsible for complying with paragraphs (4) to (6) in substitution for the person conveying the gas, and paragraph (6) shall have effect as if the reference to the person conveying gas having reasonable cause to suspect that the gas has entered or may enter premises were a reference to the appointee having such cause.

52   Gas transporters may, if they wish, subcontract the provision of their emergency service to another competent organisation (the 'emergency service provider'). In those cases, gas transporters will need to include in their safety case particulars of the arrangements they have established for the appointment of their emergency service provider. They will also need to include details of the arrangements the emergency service provider has made to respond to

emergencies (see paragraphs 127-132). The emergency service provider will need to comply with the relevant provisions of the safety case.

(12) Where an escape of gas from a gas fitting on domestic premises has resulted in a fire or explosion, the person conveying the gas in the part of the network immediately upstream of the emergency control for the supply of gas to that fitting shall, as soon as is reasonably practicable after receiving notice of the fire or explosion, cause an investigation to be carried out so as to establish, so far as is reasonably practicable, whether the escape was from installation pipework or from an, and if so which, appliance.

(13) Where an escape of gas from a network has or was likely to have resulted in a fire or explosion, the person conveying the gas in the part of the network where the gas escaped shall, as soon as is reasonably practicable after receiving notice of the escape, cause an investigation to be carried out so as to establish the source of the escape and, so far as is reasonably practicable, the reason for it.

53   Following receipt of a notification of, or having discovered, a fire or explosion caused by a gas escape, whether upstream or downstream of the emergency control at the end of the service pipe, gas transporters or their appointed agents should conduct an investigation into the incident to establish the source of the gas leak. Before starting any investigation an assessment of the risks to people entering the site should be made. Account should be taken of, for example, the risk of further structural collapse, or secondary fires or explosions. The investigation should only be undertaken to the extent that it is safe to do so, and in so far as any damage to installation pipework and appliances allows.

54   Fires and explosions in premises can occur as a result of a leak on a main, service pipe, installation pipework or appliance. Gas transporters will, therefore, need to adopt a systematic approach to establishing whether the gas leak originated in the premises or from their pipes. Where evidence indicates the leak was on the consumer's side, gas transporters should carry out confirmatory checks. To establish whether the leak was on installation pipework, it will probably be appropriate to conduct a pressure check of the installation pipework. In conducting these tests, the investigator should record any obvious visible signs that there had been an escape of gas from an appliance, eg a gas tap left open.

55   For the purposes of the report, evidence that the taps were left open would need to be set in the context of other failures, eg leaks from installation pipework. In such circumstances it would be acceptable to record the source of the leak as installation pipework rather than the appliance. Where obvious visual signs point towards an appliance being the source of the leak, and there is an absence of any evidence of leakage on installation pipework, it will be sufficient for the purpose of the investigation to record those appliances, if any, which exhibit obvious visible signs that gas could have escaped from them.

56   Where the investigation establishes the leak was on a main or service pipe, a fuller investigation of the cause will be necessary under regulation 7(13). An investigation will also be required where a gas escape was of a sufficient scale to have made a fire or explosion likely, but had not ignited.

57   It would not be expected that a 'weeping joint' would require investigation because the scale of the leak would be unlikely to be such that a sufficiently large gas/air mixture above the lower explosive limit would accumulate in practice. However, an investigation would be expected of leaks where gas transporters, or their emergency service providers, judged it prudent

in the interests of safety to evacuate property, or in more remote areas close public highways etc.

58   Procedures detailing how investigations of fires or explosions caused by gas escapes are to be undertaken should be set down in the duty holder's safety case. The investigation should be approached systematically and the procedures should include details of the sequence of steps to be taken and how information is to be recorded. Arrangements will need to be established to ensure that investigations are undertaken by competent people.

(14)   Where an incident notifiable under regulation 6(1) of the Reporting of Injuries, Diseases and Dangerous Occurrences Regulations 1995[a] has arisen as a result of an escape of carbon monoxide gas from incomplete combustion of gas in a gas fitting, the person who supplied the gas shall, as soon as is reasonably practicable after receiving notice of the incident, cause an investigation to be carried out so as to establish, so far as is reasonably practicable, the cause of the escape and accumulation of the carbon monoxide gas.

(a)   SI 1995/3163.

59   Suppliers should establish procedures for receiving reports from gas transporters where a death or injury notifiable under RIDDOR has occurred as a result of exposure to CO produced by a gas fitting. The supplier will need to take steps to identify both the circumstances that led to the escape of CO, and the reasons why it built up to such an extent that a death or major injury resulted. If the supplier does not have the necessary expertise, a third party may be appointed to undertake the investigation. The duty holder will need to be satisfied that the third party is competent to carry out the investigation. Arrangements should also be made for a scientific investigation to be carried out where appropriate. Those undertaking scientific work need not be CORGI registered but where it is necessary to break gas ways, or otherwise to do work on gas fittings, eg removal of an appliance, they should be accompanied by someone who is.

(15)   Where a person who conveys gas receives notice of an incident referred to in paragraph (14), he shall, as soon as is reasonably practicable, inform the relevant gas supplier of that fact.

60   Gas transporters will need to establish arrangements to ensure that details of incidents notifiable under regulation 6(1) of RIDDOR, caused as a result of an escape of CO, are passed to the relevant supplier promptly and accurately. This information should be consistent with that provided to HSE in the RIDDOR report. Contact points will need to be established and kept up to date.

(16)   A person who causes an investigation to be carried out pursuant to paragraphs (12), (13) or (14) shall -

(a)   ensure that the individuals who carry it out are competent;

(b)   notify the Executive before the investigation begins of the intention to carry it out;

(c)   ensure that a report of the investigation is prepared and a copy of it is sent to the Executive as soon as is reasonably practicable after the investigation has been completed.

61   Investigating incidents is specialised work. It is important that duty holders establish arrangements to ensure that they are carried out only by people with the necessary skills, knowledge and expertise.

62   Once a situation is made safe, it is important that HSE is informed before any evidence is disturbed. The purpose of this is to provide HSE with the opportunity, if appropriate, to carry out its own investigation.

63   The duty holder is required to send a copy of the completed investigation report to HSE. This should be done irrespective of whether HSE has carried out its own investigation. The report should provide a brief description of the incident, details of the causal factors and of any remedial action taken or proposed, which may be appropriate.

(17)   In this regulation -

(a)   "the responsible person" has the same meaning as in regulation 2(1) of the 1994 Regulations;

64   'The responsible person', in relation to any premises, means the occupier of the premises, or where there is no occupier, or the occupier is away, the owner of the premises or any other person with authority to take appropriate action in relation to any gas fitting in those premises, eg the landlord or the managing agent.

(b)   any reference to an escape of gas from a gas fitting includes a reference to an escape or emission of carbon monoxide gas resulting from incomplete combustion of gas in such a fitting;

65   The requirements of regulation 7 apply both to escapes of gas, and to suspected or actual emission of CO from gas appliances.

(c)   any reference to a fire or explosion of gas is a reference to an unintended fire or explosion of gas;

(d)   any reference to a person supplying gas does not include a reference to a person to whom the gas is supplied and who provides it for use in a flat or part of premises let by him.

66   Landlords of flats, or parts of buildings, or parts of premises (eg individual holiday homes at holiday parks) which they own, may provide gas to secondary meters from their own primary meter. They are neither gas transporters nor suppliers within the meaning of these Regulations and none of the duties which relate to such people under these Regulations apply to landlords who provide this type of secondary supply. Under sub-deduct arrangements the supplier will be the person who supplies at the sub-deduct meter (see Network Code, section G1).

Content and other characteristics of gas

(1)   No person shall, subject to paragraphs (2) to (4), convey gas in a network unless the gas conforms with the requirements specified in Part I of Schedule 3.

(2)   The network emergency co-ordinator may, where it is necessary to prevent a supply emergency and in accordance with the arrangements specified in his safety case pursuant to paragraph 3(d) of Schedule 2, authorise, for the period specified in the authorisation, gas not conforming with the requirements specified in Part I of Schedule 3 to be conveyed in the network if the gas conforms with the requirements specified in Part II of that Schedule.

67   The Regulations recognise that in some circumstances the introduction of out-of-specification gas into the network is less undesirable in safety terms than

the loss of supply. Where the network emergency co-ordinator (NEC) identifies a forthcoming supply emergency or where one already exists, he may, in order to avoid the need for gas transporters to direct consumers to cease using gas, authorise gas transporters to convey gas which falls outside the normal specifications. Part II of Schedule 3 sets down the specification limits of the gas which may be authorised by the NEC.

(3)   An authorisation under paragraph (2) may be given orally or in writing and may be withdrawn at any time.

68   Depending on the circumstances, eg the speed at which an emergency develops, the NEC may authorise gas transporters orally or in writing. It will generally be helpful for the safe management of an emergency if the NEC gives some indication to gas transporters of the likely time the authorisation will remain in place. To avoid doubt, and to assist gas transporters in co-ordinating the actions of others, eg producers, terminal operators and shippers, it may be prudent to confirm oral authorisations in writing, eg by fax.

(4)   Where only one person conveys gas in a network, he may, where it is necessary to prevent a supply emergency and in accordance with the arrangements specified in his safety case pursuant to paragraph 19 of Schedule 1, convey gas which does not conform with the requirements specified in Part I of Schedule 3 if the gas conforms with the requirements specified in Part II of that Schedule.

69   Where, because there is only one gas transporter on the network, there is no NEC, that gas transporter may convey out-of-specification gas through his pipes in the event of a supply emergency (see paragraph 67). This out-of-specification gas must, however, conform with the limits set out in Part II of Schedule 3.

(5)   A person who conveys gas in a network shall ensure that suitable and sufficient tests are carried out to ensure that the gas conforms with the requirements of paragraphs (1), (2) or (4), as appropriate.

70   To demonstrate that gas being transported meets the composition requirements, appropriate tests need to be carried out. Gas transporters should establish the criteria for these tests and who will conduct them. Use can be made of test data provided by third parties provided that data is relevant and procedures have been established to monitor its validity.

71   The results of the tests should be kept in accordance with regulation 9(1)(g).

Keeping of documents

(1)   A person who prepares a safety case pursuant to these Regulations shall -

(a)   ensure that when the safety case is sent to the Executive for acceptance it is notified of an address in Great Britain for the purposes of sub-paragraphs (b) to (f) below;

(b)   keep the accepted safety case and any revision thereof or a copy thereof at that address;

(c)   keep each audit report made by him or a copy thereof at that address;

(d)   ensure that a record is made of any action taken in consequence of such an audit report and keep that record or a copy thereof at that address;

(e)   ensure that a report is made of every review carried out by him pursuant to regulation 4(3) and ensure that a copy is sent to the Executive;

(f)   keep such report or a copy thereof at that address; and

(g)   ensure that a record is made of every test carried out pursuant to regulations 8(5) and 10(6) in relation to gas he conveys and keep that record or a copy thereof at that address.

(2)   Each report and record required to be kept by paragraph (1) shall be kept for a period of 3 years after it has been made, and the safety case and revision shall be kept for so long as it is current.

(3)   It shall be sufficient compliance with paragraph (1) for the information in the documents to be kept at the address notified on film or by electronic means provided that the information is capable of being reproduced as a written copy at that address and it is secure from loss or unauthorised interference.

(4)   Where a person has notified an address pursuant to sub-paragraph (a) of paragraph (1), he may notify to the Executive a different address in Great Britain for the purposes of the provisions referred to in that sub-paragraph, and where he does so references in those provisions and in paragraph (3) where applicable to the address notified shall be construed as the address in the last notification made under this paragraph.

(5)   In this regulation "audit report" means a report made pursuant to the arrangements referred to in paragraph 11 of Schedule 1 or paragraph 4 of Schedule 2 (to the extent that the later mentioned paragraph relates to arrangements for audit).

72   An accepted safety case will be an important reference document for both management and safety representatives; and for those who have to co-operate with the gas transporter (see also paragraphs 33-37) and might be a starting point for inspection by HSE. It is important, therefore, that copies of the safety case and particulars relevant to it are kept readily available. Similarly, any audit report should include a written statement recording the main findings and recommendations of the report, and the proposed action plan.

73   Where information is kept on film or by electronic means, arrangements will need to be established to ensure that it can be easily accessed, read and copied by all those who have a legitimate need, including safety representatives and HSE inspectors. Procedures will also need to be established for revising and updating the information such that only authorised changes are made, and all copies are simultaneously amended.

Transitional provisions

(1)   Where a person conveys gas in a network before 1st April 1997 it shall be sufficient compliance by him of regulation 3(1)(a) if -

(a)   the safety case referred to therein is prepared and sent to the Executive by 30th November 1996; and

(b)   the Executive accepts the safety case by 1st April 1997.

(2)   The absence of acceptance by the Executive of a safety case prepared pursuant to regulation 3(1)(a) shall not prevent the conveyance of gas between the time of sending the safety case to the Executive and 1st April 1997.

74   A gas transporter who submits a safety case to HSE by 30 November 1996 may continue to convey gas without it being accepted by HSE until 1 April 1997. Between 30 November 1996 and 31 March 1997 gas transporters may bring into operation new additions to the network which require a safety case, on condition they have first submitted a safety case to HSE.

(3)   *Regulation 3(1)(b) need not be complied with until 31st October 1996 if on 1st April 1996 a single person who is willing to act as the network emergency co-ordinator for the network has been appointed for that purpose by all persons conveying gas in the network on 1st April 1996.*

75   If the network does not have an NEC in place on 1 April 1996, gas transporters on the network will need to appoint a prospective NEC in writing on that date.

(4)   *A person appointed pursuant to paragraph (3) shall by 31st July 1996 prepare and send to the Executive a safety case containing the particulars specified in Schedule 2.*

(5)   *Nothing in paragraph (3) shall prevent a person who conveys gas in the network from being appointed under that paragraph.*

(6)   *A person who conveys gas in a network shall, until 31st October 1996, ensure that suitable and sufficient tests are carried out to ensure that the Gas Quality Regulations 1983*[(a)] *are complied with in relation to that gas.*

(a) *SI 1983/363.*

Exemptions

(1)   *Subject to paragraph (2), the Executive may, by a certificate in writing, exempt any person or class of persons from any requirement or prohibition imposed by these Regulations, and any such exemption may be granted subject to conditions and to a limit of time and may be revoked at any time by a certificate in writing.*

(2)   *The Executive shall not grant any such exemption unless, having regard to the circumstances of the case and in particular to -*

(a)   *the conditions, if any, which it proposes to attach to the exemption; and*

(b)   *any other requirements imposed by or under any enactment which apply to the case;*

it is satisfied that the health and safety of persons likely to be affected by the exemption, will not be prejudiced in consequence of it.

Repeals, revocations and amendment

(1)   *Section 16 of the Gas Act 1986*[(b)] *is hereby repealed.*

(2)   *Paragraphs 20 and 21 of Schedule 2B to the Gas Act 1986 are hereby repealed.*

(3)   *The Gas Quality Regulations 1972*[(c)] *are hereby revoked.*

(b) *1986 c.44; section 16 and Schedule 2B were substituted by paragraph 12 of Schedule 3 and by Schedule 2 to the Gas Act 1995, respectively.*
(c) *SI 1972/1804.*

(4)   Notwithstanding paragraph (1), the Gas Quality Regulations 1983[a] shall continue in force until 31st October 1996 when they shall be revoked.

(5)   For paragraph (7) of regulation 36 of the 1994 Regulations there shall be substituted the following paragraph -

> *"(7) Nothing in paragraphs (1) to (6) above shall apply to an escape of gas from a network (within the meaning of regulation 2 of the Gas Safety (Management) Regulations 1996) or from a gas fitting supplied with gas from a network."*

(a) *SI 1983/363.*

Content of safety cases: general guidance

Main elements of a safety case

76   Safety cases should contain sufficient information to demonstrate that the duty holder's operations are safe and that the risks to the public and employees are as low as reasonably practicable. Safety cases will not be considered for acceptance unless they contain all the particulars specified in the relevant Schedules. The format of the safety case is for the gas transporter to decide, but it will be helpful to HSE if the material is structured in the following way:

(a)   factual information about the operation;

(b)   the arrangements, assessments and other details required by the Schedules, including those relating to the management system, its audit, assessment of risks and risk control measures, and arrangements for handling supply emergencies;

(c)   a summary covering the main features of (b) above.

77   If a gas transporter has more than one pipeline system connected to the network, a separate safety case for each will need to be submitted to and accepted by HSE. Where the operations are broadly similar, each safety case is expected to contain similar material.

78   The amount of detail which needs to be included in the safety case will depend on the complexity of that part of the network being considered. Clearly, where the relevant part of the network is used to convey gas only to one or two industrial operations or to a simple domestic system, eg a housing estate, the safety case will not need to be either substantial or complicated.

Co-operation between gas transporters and other duty holders

79   A gas transporter's safety case needs to address the risks which are presented by the interfaces between his operations and the activities of other gas transporters etc. In preparing or revising a safety case, the gas transporter should, therefore, consult other parties as far as is necessary to ensure that the safe management of the flow of gas is properly managed at the interfaces, and that there are adequate arrangements for dealing with gas leaks close to the boundary of two (or more) parts of the network. The parties will need to be sure that the various activities are compatible with each other and that, taken together, the management arrangements and operational measures will result in effective control of the risks.

80   Regulation 6(2) places a duty on gas transporters, the network emergency co-ordinator, holders of a licence issued under section 7A of the Gas Act 1986, producers, terminal and storage operators and others to co-operate with each other to maintain safety across the network. It will be important for gas transporters to come to workable agreements and operational arrangements with these duty holders to maintain safety on their part of the network, and enable them to conform with their respective safety cases. In establishing these arrangements consideration should be given to the extent and manner in which each party is able to contribute to the safe flow of gas, and for which it is appropriate for them to do so, taking into account the extent to which the matters concerned are properly within their control. The details of these arrangements should be set down in the gas transporter's safety case.

References to other documentation

81   The safety case should, where appropriate, refer clearly to supporting detail contained in other company documents (eg operating procedures). HSE may subsequently ask to see such supporting documentation where this is necessary to verify certain aspects of the safety case.

82   The division between the material to be included in the safety case, and any additional supporting documentation which can be provided to HSE on request, must ultimately be a matter of judgement. HSE may, if it considers that the safety case is insufficiently detailed, request further information be included in the safety case itself. As a guiding principle, the safety case should be presented as a self-contained document which:

(a)   sets out clearly the safety principles the duty holders will adopt in order to discharge their duties under these Regulations; and

(b)   includes sufficient detail to lend conviction to those principles, enabling requests for supporting documentation to be the exception rather than the rule. Accordingly, where the safety case refers to other documents, a summary of their contents should be included where appropriate and practicable.

Assessment of safety cases

83   HSE will make public the administrative arrangements, procedures and timetable for assessing safety cases. Assessment procedures will be designed to facilitate timely discussion between HSE and gas transporters, leading to agreement on any necessary changes that may be needed. These might include, for example, additional information or analysis, or actual improvements required to establish a satisfactory case for safety.

84   The procedures will include a requirement for HSE to provide in writing reasons for not accepting a safety case. A safety case will not be rejected without the gas transporter first having been given the opportunity to rectify any issues raised by HSE. Any gas transporter whose safety case is rejected will be able to appeal against that decision. It is expected that this arrangement will rarely, if ever, need to be used.

Access to accepted safety cases

85   Once a safety case has been accepted, it will provide an important reference for management, safety representatives and safety committees. It may also provide the starting point for inspection by HSE. When any revision is made, it is important that the latest version of the safety case is always easily identifiable and accessible. One way of ensuring this is routinely to incorporate all amendments into the safety case as they are made, rather than to keep them separate. It will be important to ensure that other parties, who have duties to co-operate with the gas transporter to fulfil the arrangements set down in the safety case, also have access to the relevant parts of the safety case and are kept informed of any amendments (see paragraph 80). In accordance with regulation 4(2), where revisions have a material affect on the safety case, the current revised safety case, or its relevant part, should be resubmitted to HSE for acceptance. The changes should not be implemented until the revised safety case, or relevant part, has been accepted by HSE (see paragraphs 26-29).

Other associated legislation

86   The Gas Safety (Management) Regulations 1996 (GS(M)R) are concerned essentially with the safe management of the flow of gas through the

23

network. It is not intended that the requirements of Schedule 1 to these Regulations should duplicate those required by the Pipelines Safety Regulations 1996 (PSR). PSR covers all pipelines conveying hazardous fluids, including gas pipes, and is intended to address the integrity of pipelines by ensuring their safe design, construction and installation, operation, maintenance and abandonment.

87   However, there are some areas of unavoidable overlap between these two sets of Regulations - which we have sought to keep to an absolute minimum - in particular duties dealing with management systems, operation of pipelines and response to emergencies. Although PSR covers management systems, eg in the context of the requirement for a major accident prevention document, such systems are concerned solely with pipeline integrity and consequences of its loss.

88   The safe operation duties in PSR relate to the drawing up of safe operating parameters which reflect pipeline design; and ensuring that pipelines are operated and controlled within these limits.

89   The requirement in PSR to make suitable arrangements for emergencies is to ensure that these are in place to limit any loss of containment and deal specifically with major accident hazards. GS(M)R, on the other hand, requires an effective emergency response service to be in place to deal with reports of gas escapes, either from the network or from gas fittings in consumers' premises. The arrangements under GS(M)R should particularly focus on local and domestic situations; although incident investigation should deal with all leaks which caused, or which gave rise to a significant risk of, fire or explosion.

90   To minimise duplication, those parts of any documents which are required under PSR, and which are relevant to the duties under GS(M)R, may be referred to in the GS(M)R safety case.

Particulars to be included in safety case of a person conveying gas

Regulation 3(1)

General

1   Name and address of the person preparing the safety case (in this Schedule referred to as "the duty holder").

2   A description of the operation intended to be undertaken by the duty holder.

3   A general description of the plant and premises the duty holder intends to use in connection with the operation including, in particular, the geographical location where any pipes he uses join pipes used by other persons for conveying gas.

91   The particulars required by paragraphs 1 to 3 of Schedule 1 to these Regulations are intended to provide the essential factual, or background, information about the transporter which HSE needs in order properly to assess the safety case. The information should be presented in a logical manner and, as far as possible, be self-supporting.

Description of the operation

92   The description of the operation should cover all operational characteristics which help to identify risks associated with the management of the flow of gas and which provide a proper understanding of the organisational arrangements set out in the safety case. Where relevant this should, for example, include information about:

(a)   the purpose of the pipeline;

(b)   total length of the different types of pipeline in that part of the network;

(c)   volumes of gas likely to be conveyed through such pipelines, the pressure at which the pipeline is designed to operate, eg high pressure (>7 barg), an indication of the location of interruptible consumers and other very large volume consumers; and

(d)   capacity constraints of such pipelines.

It may be sufficient simply to provide a high level summary with reference to supporting documents.

93   The description should, where relevant and feasible, be supported by plans or diagrams which clearly delineate geographical boundaries. The location of safety critical plant and equipment, terminal and storage facilities (on and offshore) and interfaces with other pipeline and storage systems also need to be provided. Where such interfaces are identified, the name of the operator needs to be provided. The safety case should set out the arrangements established to ensure that design and planning criteria are kept up to date, taking account of changes in the patterns of gas consumption, so that gas can continue to flow safely through the duty holder's pipes at all times.

94   The description needs to include details of the control centres established to ensure the safe flow of gas, their geographical location and the boundaries of their area. The means of communication between such centres and terminal and storage operators, other pipeline operators having interfaces with the gas

transporter producing the safety case, and the network emergency co-ordinator (NEC), should be included.

95   Where provided, plans or diagrams should be drawn to a scale suitable for the easy identification of key features of the undertaking associated with the safe management of gas flow.

4   Particulars of any -

(a)   technical specifications;

(b)   procedures or arrangements relating to operation and maintenance,

which the duty holder intends to follow in connection with the operation he intends to undertake insofar as they affect the health and safety of persons.

96   It will be sufficient for the safety case to refer to internal or recognised technical specifications or standards (eg BSI, CEN, ISO, or industry publications such as IGE Recommendations) which the gas transporter intends to follow in relation to managing the safe flow of gas through his part of the network, rather than describe them in detail.

97   Technical specifications or standards need to be restricted to those concerned with the reliability of safety critical plant and 'software', eg management of the safe flow of gas, or provision of an effective emergency service. The use of the term 'software' in this guidance does not mean computer programs and applications, but rather it refers to the management and control arrangements duty holders have in place to discharge their duties under these Regulations, including appropriate quality standards (eg BS 5750/ISO 9000). However, any technical specifications or standards relating to IT applications need to be cited where appropriate. The safety case needs to include an adequate explanation of how these standards and specifications are implemented and complied with.

Operational and maintenance procedures

98   Operational and maintenance procedures should also be addressed. All that is required is a high level description, and reference need only be made to existing written procedures, which are not covered by more specific requirements elsewhere in this Schedule. These might include here or elsewhere:

(a)   management of the flow of gas through the duty holder's part of the network;

(b)   operation of associated plant, to the extent this might affect the safe flow of gas through the duty holder's pipelines;

(c)   maintenance of the flow of gas in the event of plant breakdown;

(d)   how safety inspections and planned preventive maintenance (involving, for example, closing down parts of the network) might affect the flow of gas; and how continuity of supply will be secured. Details should also be included on how planned, or unplanned, maintenance activities will be communicated to others who may be affected by them;

(e)   dealing with reported gas leaks (both upstream and downstream of the consumer's emergency control valve) and reports of possible CO emission;

(f)   management and operation of interfaces with other gas transporters;

(g)   audit arrangements;

(h)   liaison with enforcing authorities and emergency services; and

(i)   appointment, training and ongoing assessment of the competence of safety critical staff, eg control room operators, system controllers.

Safety management

5   *A statement of the significant findings of the risk assessment he has made pursuant to regulation 3 of the Management of Health and Safety at Work Regulations 1992(a), and particulars of the arrangements he has made in accordance with regulation 4(1) thereof.*

(a) SI 1992/2051.

Risk assessment

99   The Management of Health and Safety at Work Regulations 1992 (MHSWR) require employers and self-employed people to make a suitable and sufficient assessment of the risks to the health and safety of their employees and others, including the public, who may be affected by their undertaking. However, in the context of the safety case, the significant findings of the risk assessment and preventive measures should include only those that may affect the safe management of the flow of gas, and the provision of an emergency response service. The assessment should be reviewed whenever there is reason to suspect it is no longer valid, or where there has been a significant change in the matters to which it relates. The particulars of the risk assessment, and the preventive measures required, should be included in the safety case whether or not the gas transporter employs fewer than five employees.

100   The risk assessment should identify foreseeable events and take into account such events identified under paragraph 3(a) of Schedule 2 of these Regulations, which form part of the NEC's safety case. This will include events which may affect many people at a time but occur infrequently (such as the loss of supply to domestic customers, or a major leak on a transmission or distribution main). It will be important to identify such events, the risks they present, and the different circumstances in which they might occur.

101   Risk assessments should be reviewed periodically, modified as appropriate, and consequential amendments made to the safety case. The interval between reviews will depend on the nature of the hazards and the degree of risk that the change in operations is likely to produce. As a minimum, it will be necessary to conduct the reassessment as part of the three-year review of the safety case, as required under regulation 4(3).

Health and safety arrangements

102   The preventive and protective measures which need to be taken will depend on the results of the risk assessment under normal operations, operations during maintenance or planned changes from the norm (eg temporary reduction in pressure/capacity of the pipelines), and all foreseeable supply emergencies or other abnormal events. Paragraph 27 of the Approved Code of Practice to MHSWR sets out useful principles in determining when, and what, protective and preventive measures need to be taken.

103   The gas transporter's safety case should indicate the form in which these detailed procedures and protective measures are documented, and the

arrangements for making them available to managers, supervisors, other employees, safety representatives and safety committees.

6   Particulars to demonstrate that the management system of the duty holder is adequate to ensure that the relevant statutory provisions will (in respect of matters within his control) be complied with in relation to the operation he intends to undertake.

104   The term 'management system' means the organisation and arrangements established by the duty holder to manage his undertaking (see paragraph 22(b) of Schedule 1 to these Regulations).

105   Each safety case should include particulars to demonstrate that the management system is capable of controlling safely the flow of gas in that part of the network subject to the safety case. For example, the safety case should refer to the arrangements established to manage any interfaces with other parts of the network, terminal and storage operators and other users of the network, eg shippers and suppliers under normal, emergency or other abnormal circumstances. It is not necessary to address here those aspects of the operation which are required under paragraphs 12-20 of Schedule 1 to these Regulations.

Monitoring of health and safety performance

106   Effective monitoring should be an integral part of the safety management system; health and safety performance should be monitored in the same way, and with the same rigour, as business performance. The safety case should describe the arrangements for monitoring progress towards achievement of the health and safety objectives of the safe management of the flow of gas, and the provision of an effective emergency service. The system for internal monitoring, and for reporting and recording abnormal events, should be described in the safety case. This should include the means of feeding back lessons learnt to others who may have been involved or affected by the duty holder's operations; for example, those who use the duty holder's part of the network (ie shippers and suppliers), or those connected to it (ie other gas transporters, terminal and storage operators). Consideration should be given to the consequential updating of documentation and procedures, eg the Network Code, Local Operating Procedures etc.

107   Monitoring should be carried out by suitable personnel at prescribed intervals assisted, as necessary, by other competent people. Managers are responsible for monitoring compliance with those standards for which they are responsible.

HSE guidance

108   Guidance on effective management of health and safety is contained in two HSE publications, *Successful health and safety management* (ISBN 0 7176 0425 X) and *Human factors in industrial safety* (ISBN 0 7176 0472 1).

7   Particulars to demonstrate that the duty holder has established adequate arrangements for ensuring the competence of his employees in health and safety matters.

Competence and training

109   The Health and Safety at Work etc Act 1974 (HSW Act) and MHSWR require all employers to ensure that employees are competent to carry out their tasks safely. Competence means that employees have the necessary skills, experience, knowledge and personal qualities. Gas transporters will need to

identify essential competence requirements, and ensure, through staff selection criteria, provision of necessary information, instruction, training and supervision that the demands of a task do not exceed an individual's ability to carry it out such that he creates risks to the health and safety of himself or others.

110   Requirements for competence, and the means of acquiring it (including, where appropriate, specifying standards of training or qualifications), will need to be determined in the light of the MHSWR risk assessment. Consideration should be given to competence requirements where a change in the nature of the work is proposed. Refresher training should be considered and provided, as necessary, on an ongoing basis.

111   The safety case needs to describe the general arrangements made by the gas transporter to ensure that employees are competent as regards the safe management of the flow of gas, and in providing an effective emergency response service. This applies to all employees, whether they are involved in managerial, supervisory or operational tasks. Particular mention might need to be made of the arrangements for ensuring the competence of safety critical staff, eg control room operators, who have to deal effectively with supply emergencies, or those responsible for controlling major gas escapes from the network.

8   *Particulars to demonstrate that the duty holder has established adequate arrangements for managing work carried out by persons who are not his employees on or in relation to plant or premises which he owns or controls.*

Contractors

112   The safety case needs to describe arrangements for managing work which has been contracted out in so far as the arrangements concern the safe management of the flow of gas, or provision of an effective emergency response service. Selection criteria, monitoring and review of performance against agreed objectives need to be described, as do the criteria for the termination of a contract on health and safety grounds. The arrangements will need to ensure that:

(a)   contractors have a management system in place which is both capable of meeting safety objectives and consistent with the duty holder's system;

(b)   the division of responsibility between the gas transporter and the contractor for specific aspects of safety management is clearly defined;

(c)   contractors draw up and follow safe systems of work which include the provision and use of suitable plant and equipment;

(d)   contractors' employees are sufficient in number, competent and trained to an appropriate standard; and

(e)   adequate supervision is provided where necessary (either by the contractor, or the duty holder).

9   *Particulars to demonstrate that the duty holder has established adequate arrangements for passing information relevant to health and safety to persons within his undertaking.*

113   Each safety case should describe the arrangements the duty holder has established for the provision of sufficient information to enable the safe management of the flow of gas on that part of the network, and for dealing with

supply emergencies and gas escapes, including the escape or emission of CO from appliances. The HSW Act and MHSWR place duties on employers to provide their employees, contractors and others who may be affected by their undertakings (eg the public) with information sufficient to ensure their health and safety. MHSWR place a duty on every employee to inform their employer, or a fellow employee with specific responsibility for health and safety, of any serious and immediate danger, and of shortcomings in the employer's arrangements for safety. The safety case needs to describe the arrangements the gas transporter has in place to ensure that such information, in so far as it relates to the safe management of the flow of gas or provision of an emergency response service, is passed by employees to line managers (or to safety advisers or safety officers, as appropriate), and that action is taken on receipt of such information.

114 High standards of health and safety performance cannot be achieved without the positive and informed commitment of the workforce. Arrangements for consulting employees should be consistent with requirements under the Safety Representatives and Safety Committees Regulations 1977, or other statutory requirements for consultation which the Health and Safety Commission may bring forward.

115 The safety case should give details of systems, including IT systems, which are in place to enable the necessary flow of information to all employees, and others who need access to it, to maintain the safe management of the flow of gas, or the provision of an effective emergency response service.

10 Particulars to demonstrate that the duty holder has established adequate arrangements for passing and receiving information relevant to health and safety to and from other persons who have duties under these Regulations.

116 Effective arrangements are also needed to ensure that information relevant to the safe management of the flow of gas, or provision of an effective emergency response service, is exchanged in a timely manner between the duty holder and others who have duties under these Regulations, including other gas transporters, shippers, suppliers, terminal and storage operators, producers, and the NEC. This will enable duty holders to discharge their duties under these Regulations and the arrangements should be set out in the safety case. The safety case should also set out the arrangements for dealing with members of the public and consumers, including those with interruptible contracts, in the event of a supply emergency or gas escape from the network. Where it is more appropriate to set out the detail of specific information exchange arrangements under other paragraphs in Schedule 1, there is no need to do so here.

117 It is essential that those who have duties to co-operate with gas transporters are made aware of the arrangements described in the safety case which are relevant to them.

11 Particulars to demonstrate that the duty holder has established adequate arrangements for audit and the making of any necessary reports.

Audit

118 Paragraph 11 of Schedule 1 requires gas transporters to include in their safety cases sufficient details to demonstrate that they have established adequate arrangements to audit those parts of the management system which deal with the safe management of the flow of gas and provision of an emergency response service. The terms 'audit' and 'management system' are defined in paragraph 22 of Schedule 1.

119 Audit is also referred to in the HSE publication *Successful health and safety management* as the structured process of collecting independent information and drawing up plans for corrective action. This independent audit process constitutes the final stage in the management control cycle, providing the necessary feedback to corporate management to enable the undertaking to maintain and improve its health and safety performance. As with other aspects of the management system, performance standards for the audit and review process should be set, communicated to those who need to know, and monitored.

120 In order to provide the necessary independent perspective and maximise the benefits from the audit process, audits need to be carried out by competent people from outside the line management chain responsible for the areas or activities being audited, or by external consultants.

121 There may be particular value in conducting audits shortly (perhaps six months or so) after a significant change in management arrangements, including such changes (where the gas transporter is a subsidiary company or operating unit) in the parent company or where a material change has required a revised safety case to be submitted to and accepted by HSE.

122 Any changes to management arrangements resulting from the audit need to be reflected in the safety case and supporting documentation.

Co-operation

12   Particulars of the arrangements the duty holder has established to enable him to comply with regulation 6 (co-operation) including (except where he is the network emergency co-ordinator) particulars of the arrangements he has established to ensure that any directions given to him by the network emergency co-ordinator are followed.

123 Each safety case needs to set down the working arrangements and operational procedures the duty holder has established with those who have duties under regulation 6(2), eg producers, other gas transporters, shippers, suppliers, terminal and storage operators, and the NEC, to enable each party to comply with the Regulations, and the safety case. The arrangements should address normal operating conditions, local and national supply emergencies, and where gas escapes are reported close to the boundary with respective gas transporters (or their emergency service providers).

124 In addition, the safety case should include here other matters not addressed elsewhere. These might include, for example, the provision of information to gas transporters about certain consumers regarding the ability of gas transporters to interrupt their supply; arrangements suppliers have established to ensure their consumers follow the directions to cease using gas when directed by a gas transporter; and arrangements for developing new procedures, amending the Network Code and Local Operating Procedures, co-ordination of training and conducting emergency exercises etc.

Gas escapes and investigations

13   Particulars of the arrangements -

(a)   the duty holder and any emergency service provider appointed by him have established to enable him or the provider, as the case may be, to comply with regulation 7(4) to (6);

(b)   the duty holder has established to appoint emergency service providers.

Liaison with British Gas plc

125 British Gas plc will provide a national 0800 emergency freephone number for use by the public, consumers and the emergency services in the event of an actual or suspected gas leak, emission of CO or a fire or explosion where a gas escape is thought to be the cause. BG plc will need to be able to relay calls immediately to the emergency service provider for each area. To enable it to do so, gas transporters will need to have notified BG plc of:

(a) the parts of the network they cover; and

(b) details of the emergency service provider(s) for each part.

126 Arrangements for providing this information, and for notifying BG plc immediately of any changes, should be described in the safety case.

127 The safety case should also describe arrangements for:

(a) recording notifications of emergencies received from BG plc and action taken in response to each one, including the time taken to make safe;

(b) informing BG plc of any escape of gas occurring as a consequence of planned work, in case the escape is reported by members of the public in the vicinity; and

(c) audit trails to ensure that there has been no delay in receiving/forwarding notifications of emergencies and actions taken to deal with them.

Receiving direct emergency calls

128 Although BG plc will provide the national emergency freephone number, there may be occasions when consumers will report emergencies directly to gas transporters, or their emergency service provider. The safety case should, therefore, describe the arrangements to:

(a) notify BG plc of all emergency calls received directly, including where the duty holder has appointed a third party emergency service provider; and

(b) ensure that action is taken to respond to the emergency (if it is the responsibility of the duty holder) without waiting for directions to do so from BG plc.

Dealing with reported gas escapes

129 The safety case needs to include details of the procedures and arrangements to be followed to ensure that emergencies are dealt with promptly and effectively. Those details should include the following:

(a) arrangements for ensuring an adequate 24-hour response to reports of gas escapes;

(b) procedures for determining the source of the gas escape or CO emission; and

(c) how gas escapes will be dealt with:

    (i) upstream of the service pipe, including arrangements for liaison and working with other gas transporters where gas escapes are near boundaries on the network; and

(ii)   downstream of the service pipe (ie gas fittings and installation pipework).

130   Arrangements for dealing with all foreseeable types of gas escapes identified by the risk assessment should be described in the safety case. The action required will vary according to the scale of the gas escape, the geographical area affected and the duration of the incident. In describing the arrangements, the following factors should be taken into account:

(a)   procedures for controlling, directing and monitoring the situation from initial response to reinstatement of normal services. This may include the establishment of an incident control centre;

(b)   arrangements for minimising the need to discontinue supply to consumers;

(c)   competence, skills and experience of all operatives, in particular those of contractors;

(d)   training of operatives to deal with major gas escapes, eg those affecting several streets, escapes at night etc;

(e)   availability of sufficient numbers of operatives, with appropriate rights of entry powers, when needed;

(f)   procedures for ensuring effective communication with affected consumers;

(g)   where necessary, arrangements for discontinuing and reinstating supplies to consumers' premises. These arrangements will need to include procedures for ensuring systematic coverage of all premises in the affected area and checks on all appliances for obvious visible signs of spillage of the products of combustion when appliances are relit;

(h)   liaison with other gas transporters/emergency service providers in the event of gas escapes close to boundaries between different parts of the network;

(i)   arrangements for liaison/co-operation with the local fire and other emergency services, in particular where there has been a fire in premises to which gas is supplied, or there is a major leak from a local distribution main; and

(j)   arrangements for liaising with gas suppliers about the needs of their vulnerable consumers; and with local authorities and care organisations in the affected area, for providing emergency shelter etc in the event that premises need to be evacuated.

Reports of suspected escapes of CO from appliances

131   The safety case will need to describe the arrangements for dealing with reports of suspected escapes of CO. These will include procedures for identifying, where this is possible, the source of the escape or emission of CO and the steps to be taken to make safe, including disconnection procedures where appropriate. It is recognised that appliances which are spilling the products of combustion may not do so under all atmospheric conditions. The safety case should describe the procedures for taking this fact into account in establishing whether it is possible to identify if an appliance is spilling the products of combustion. The safety case will also need to set down the

33

arrangements for passing information to the relevant supplier where an escape of CO has resulted in a death or major injury notifiable under RIDDOR. This should include, for example, procedures for establishing and maintaining an up-to-date list of supplier contacts, and for recording information passed to them.

132 Where a gas transporter or emergency service provider identifies a dangerous appliance while attending a gas escape, or relighting appliances following reinstatement of supply to the premises, he should offer to disconnect the appliance, but has no legal power to do so under these Regulations if the occupant refuses. However, the gas transporter (or emergency service provider) has powers of entry to premises to deal with dangerous appliances. In such circumstances where the consumer does not agree to the voluntary disconnection of the dangerous appliance, it would be appropriate to exercise the rights of entry to disconnect the appliance from the installation pipework. The gas transporter should make a report on the dangerous appliance to HSE, where required under regulation 6(2) of RIDDOR and ensure the appliance is suitably labelled as being unsafe.

Appointment of an emergency service provider

133 Duty holders may choose to appoint an emergency service provider to act on their behalf to deal with reported gas leaks, or emission of CO. The safety case will need to set down the arrangements for ensuring that the emergency service provider has operatives with the necessary skills, competence and hardware to enable duty holders to demonstrate how their duties will be discharged under these Regulations. It should also describe the arrangements for ensuring there are sufficient numbers of operators with rights-of-entry powers. Details of how the emergency service provider will discharge his responsibilities under these Regulations (essentially covering the same information required under paragraphs 127-132) will also need to be included.

14 Particulars to demonstrate that the duty holder has established adequate arrangements to enable him to comply with paragraphs (12), (13), (15) and (16) of regulation 7, for co-ordinating the investigations he causes to be carried out pursuant to that regulation with other investigations carried out pursuant thereto, and for participating in such other investigations.

134 The safety case should set out the arrangements the gas transporter has made for investigating fire and explosion incidents which occur downstream of the emergency control as a result of an escape of gas, and those incidents upstream of the emergency control which have, or could have, resulted in a fire or explosion. Arrangements should be made to ensure that those who conduct the investigation, whether the gas transporter's own employees or those of a contractor, have the necessary skills, competencies and experience to do so to a satisfactory standard.

135 The safety case needs to cover the arrangements for recording factual information, conclusions reached about the cause of the incident and recommendations for any remedial action which may be appropriate. The arrangements for ensuring that such remedial action has been carried out should be described. This also applies to the dissemination of any lessons learnt from the investigation.

136 The safety case should describe the arrangements for submitting a report of the investigation to HSE.

137 The safety case will need to set out arrangements for notifying gas suppliers if emissions of CO have led to a death or injury notifiable to HSE

under regulation 6(1) of RIDDOR, and to supply all the necessary information to enable the supplier to conduct the investigation into the incident (see guidance under regulation 7(14) of these Regulations).

Content and other characteristics of gas

15   Particulars to demonstrate that the duty holder has established adequate arrangements to ensure that all gas he conveys complies with regulation 8.

138   The safety case should include particulars to demonstrate the duty holder has systems in place which ensure that only gas permitted under regulation 8 will be conveyed through his pipes. In practice the duty holder will establish a series of contracts and protocols with others relating to the conveyance of gas on their part of the network. To some extent gas transporters will be dependent on others fulfilling their obligations under these contracts and protocols, eg Network Code and Network Entry Agreements etc. The safety case should identify these relationships, and set down the arrangements for managing the interfaces. Part I of Schedule 3 sets out the content and characteristics of gas which may be conveyed under normal operating conditions.

139   The safety case should describe how the duty holder will ensure that the necessary tests to demonstrate conformity with Part I, and Part II where appropriate, of Schedule 3 are carried out. The geographical location of all testing facilities should be included in the description, together with the reasoning for particular locations being chosen. This is particularly important in respect of tests for pressure at the extremities of the duty holder's part of the network. The safety case may take account of any documentary evidence provided by other gas transporters who have transported gas to the duty holder's part of the network that the composition of gas conforms to the statutory requirements.

140   Where a blending service for gas which does not conform to the requirements of Part I of Schedule 3 is provided by a gas transporter, the safety case needs to describe the arrangements for blending, and set out the safeguards which are in place to prevent such out-of-specification gas from being consumed by consumers on the network. The safety case should also describe any arrangements the transporter has established to convey out-of-specification gas from a gas processing facility to another place where the gas is treated to bring it into conformity with the requirements of Part I of Schedule 3.

141   The safety case should explain how the duty holder will co-operate with the NEC and other gas transporters in allowing, where appropriate, gas conforming to Part II of Schedule 3 to be conveyed through the network to prevent a supply emergency or to minimise the impact of one. In particular, the safety case will need to set out the arrangements made with producers, terminal operators and shippers or other gas transporters for obtaining such gas. Details of the tests to be undertaken should also be described.

142   The safety case should describe the arrangements the transporter has put in place to provide sufficient pressure at the end of the service pipe to ensure that gas appliances which consumers might reasonably be expected to use operate safely wherever the premises are situated on the network. This should include any pressure management techniques used to deal with the expected variations in consumption between peak and normal demands throughout the year.

143   Where consumers use equipment which is liable to produce a pressure of less than one atmosphere, or might inject extraneous gases (including air) into

the duty holder's part of the network, the safety case should set out the arrangements the duty holder has to prevent this happening, eg via the Network Code. This may include the need to publicise that such equipment should be fitted with antifluctuators or non-return valves.

Continuity of supply

16   Particulars to demonstrate that the duty holder has established adequate arrangements to minimise the risk of a supply emergency.

144   To maintain safe flow, and to minimise the risk of a supply emergency, gas must be supplied to, and maintained in, the network in sufficient quantity to allow it to be pumped and routed through the network so it is delivered at the point of supply at an adequate pressure. Failure to do this may result in a drop of pressure, or a loss of supply, which could put consumers at risk. For this reason, ensuring continuity of supply lies at the heart of safe gas flow management. How continuity of supply is maintained is fundamental to the acceptance of the safety case.

145   The duty holder will in practice need to establish a series of contractual arrangements and operational procedures with others which aim to ensure continuity of supply, including security of supply criteria, and for co-operating with the NEC in allowing gas conforming to Part II of Schedule 3 into the network. The safety case should describe arrangements for meeting security of supply criteria, for example, by ensuring sufficient gas is held in store to meet the one-in-50-year winter. The safety case should also describe the procedures for monitoring changes in the gas supply market to ensure that arrangements for meeting the cold winter criterion can continue to be met.

146   For public gas transporters (PGTs) licensed under the Gas Act 1986, these arrangements will be described in their Network Code and other supporting documents, eg Local Operating Procedures and Network Entry and Exit Agreements etc. The safety case should identify these relationships, describe the procedures for managing the interfaces, and arrangements for modifying these documents. The safety case should also describe the interfaces between PGTs and other gas transporters who are exempt from the need to hold a PGT licence.

147   The safety case should also describe the arrangements for ensuring that no changes to the Network Code etc, which might give rise to material change to the safety case, can be brought into effect until a revised safety case has been submitted to, and accepted by, HSE. It will be important to consider whether a series of smaller changes to the Network Code might cumulatively give rise to a material change, requiring resubmission of the safety case.

148   The safety case should set out the arrangements the duty holder has put in place to ensure that sufficient gas is available to maintain supply to consumers on the part of the network which is the subject of the duty holder's safety case. This should include a description of the arrangements for the effective planning, organisation, control and monitoring of the management of gas flow, for example, procedures for:

(a)   forecasting long-term, medium-term, daily and within-day demand;

(b)   ensuring that demand forecast is met, obtaining gas of a suitable composition from contracts with producers, spot market, other gas transporters, storage operators etc, including, where appropriate, arrangements for blending;

Guidance

Schedule 1

Schedule

1

Guidance

Schedule 1

Schedule

1

Guidance

Schedule 1

(c) monitoring the gas flow to identify possible imbalances between supply and demand, including the arrangements for obtaining appropriate information about the availability of gas supplies; and

(d) adjusting the input of gas to maintain continuity of supply so as to prevent a supply emergency developing.

17 Particulars to demonstrate that the duty holder has established adequate arrangements to ensure that the gas he conveys will be at an adequate pressure when it leaves the part of the network used by him.

149 Where gas is provided to other gas transporters, the safety case should describe the arrangements for ensuring that gas is provided at the agreed pressures and volumes. Where this is not possible, because of an emerging or actual supply emergency within the duty holder's part of the network, the safety case should set out the arrangements for notifying the NEC, gas transporters and other users of the duty holder's part of the network, eg shippers and suppliers, who may be affected; and the action the duty holder proposes to take to rectify the situation in so far as that is possible.

150 The safety case should describe arrangements for monitoring pressure at, or in the vicinity of, any pipeline interconnection.

Supply emergencies

18 Particulars to demonstrate that the duty holder has established adequate arrangements for dealing with supply emergencies or other incidents which could endanger persons.

151 The risk assessment carried out under paragraph 4 of Schedule 1 is likely to have identified a number of circumstances which threaten the safe flow of gas in the part of the network subject to the duty holder's safety case. These foreseeable events might include, for example, failure of a major high pressure pipe, failure of safety critical equipment, an unexpected change in weather conditions, or overpressure in a distribution system. Other foreseeable events which might impact on the part of the network covered by the safety case, eg operational problems offshore or at a beach terminal, will have been identified in the NEC's safety case. The measures necessary for dealing with such events should be included in the duty holder's safety case.

152 As a first step, a clear definition of what constitutes a supply emergency needs to be established and described. Emergencies tend to fall into two types. First there are those where there is insufficient gas in a part, or parts, of the network, and no constraint on the ability to move gas into the affected area, if it is available. Such circumstances are likely to give rise to network emergencies and the NEC would have responsibility for co-ordinating the actions of gas transporters, terminal and storage operators etc (see paragraph 3(b) of Schedule 2 to these Regulations). The second type of emergency, which would not involve the NEC, is where sufficient gas is available within the network as a whole but a constraint means that it is not physically possible to move gas into the area where a supply emergency is developing. Such circumstances give rise to local emergencies and management of the situation rests with those gas transporters immediately affected.

Local supply emergencies

153 The safety case should set out the criteria to be used to declare a potential local supply emergency on the part of the network subject to the safety case, and identify other parts of the network, and the relevant gas transporters, who

might be affected. In those circumstances where other gas transporters are likely to be affected, the safety case should set out the liaison arrangements and protocols established for managing the emergency.

154 The arrangements and procedures should include the means by which any necessary reduction in gas consumption will be achieved. This should include arrangements for liaising with shippers and suppliers, and for communicating and dealing with consumers. Details of how these arrangements, and relevant information, are kept up to date should also be included.

155 Arrangements should be established for operating an emergency control centre to co-ordinate activities during an emergency. These should be set out in the safety case and might include details of the communications and computer equipment required, and the means of ensuring sufficient numbers of competent personnel are available to deal effectively with the emergency at any given time. Details of the command structure which will operate, and the roles and responsibilities of key personnel should be included. Details of the liaison arrangements with suppliers about the needs of vulnerable consumers, the local emergency services and affected local authorities should be described.

National supply emergency

156 The safety case should describe the arrangements for communicating with the NEC, for responding to his directions, and for confirming that action has been taken. If any additional procedures to those set out above are required to manage adequately a network emergency, these should also be set out in the safety case.

Other incidents

157 The safety case should address the preventive steps in place to minimise the risk of other events, identified by the risk assessment, which might threaten the safe flow of gas in the part of the network subject to the safety case. These might include, for example, the possible incorrect connection of pipes operating at different pressures, or a reduction in pressure in a distribution main because an appropriate antifluctuator was not fitted, or the inadvertent injection of gas not conforming to regulation 8(1) into the network. Where these preventive measures fail, the procedures necessary to make the situation safe, and to restore supply, should be described, unless they are covered elsewhere in the safety case. Particular attention should be paid to the arrangements for dealing with domestic consumers who might be affected.

19 Where the duty holder is the only person conveying gas in a network, particulars to demonstrate that he has established adequate arrangements to decide when and for how long gas not conforming with the requirements of regulation 8(1) should be conveyed in the network pursuant to regulation 8(4).

158 Regulation 8(4) permits the duty holder to introduce gas which conforms to Part II of Schedule 3, where this is necessary to prevent a supply emergency. The safety case should set out the criteria for determining when this provision will be exercised and the operational arrangements which have been established for introducing and controlling the flow of gas conforming to Part II of Schedule 3.

20 Without prejudice to paragraph 18 above, particulars of the procedures that the duty holder has established to discontinue safely supply to consumers, when it is known there is insufficient gas to satisfy demand.

159 The safety case should describe the criteria to be used for determining the sequence in which the supply to consumers will be discontinued. The duty holder will need to take account of the risks to consumers associated with the loss of supply of gas, in particular, domestic and other priority consumers, and its subsequent reinstatement. This is likely to require a hierarchical approach to disconnection, which takes account of risks to different groups of consumers and any priority consumer criteria established by the Secretary of State for Trade and Industry. As far as possible, the hierarchy should be based on objective engineering principles and aimed at reducing to a minimum the safety risks arising from a supply emergency across the affected parts of the network. In practice, the duty holder, and other gas transporters, will probably need to adopt a common approach across the network. The details of this should be recorded in gas transporters' safety cases, and that of the NEC.

160 Where other gas transporters may be affected by a local emergency situation, the arrangements for co-ordinating action to discontinue supply safely across the affected area should be set out in the safety case. These might include, for example, written protocols on the sequence for discontinuing supply to particular groups of consumers on different gas transporters' pipelines and, if appropriate, the control centre which will co-ordinate the emergency response (see also paragraphs 153-155).

161 The safety case should detail the procedures for ensuring that all consumers directed to cease using gas do so safely. This might involve collecting information on, for example, lead time requirements and availability of alternative energy supplies, so the period of notice given is appropriate. In the case of shipper-nominated interruptible consumers and certain priority consumers, shippers will need to satisfy the duty holder that they have carried out the necessary checks on lead times etc. The particular arrangements for the safe disconnection of domestic consumers should be set down in the safety case. These should include arrangements for communicating instructions, visits to properties where appropriate and special arrangements for vulnerable consumers. Procedures for liaising with local emergency services and affected local authorities should also be described.

162 The safety case should include details of the arrangements gas transporters have for making clear to consumers, particularly large volume consumers, their obligations to conform with any direction to cease using gas and any co-operative arrangements with shippers and suppliers to underpin these arrangements. It should also contain the procedures in place to monitor that consumers have responded to any directions given, and where they have not, the action the duty holder will take to ensure the safe management of gas flow, including any arrangements to ensure the direction to stop using gas is complied with.

163 The safety case should also describe the arrangements for determining the level of reserve gas required to ensure that in a supply emergency (whether local or national) the part of the network covered by the safety case can be safely managed, if all or part of it needs to shut down. Where reserve gas is, in effect, held by another gas transporter, the safety case should describe the arrangements between the two gas transporters to ensure both parts of the network can be shut down safely.

21 *Particulars of the procedures that the duty holder has established to restore safely the gas supply to consumers, following an interruption in supply.*

164 The safety case should set out the criteria for declaring when a local supply emergency is over and the arrangements for ensuring continuing co-operation between affected gas transporters. The safety case should describe

the arrangements for reinstating supply safely following either a local or national emergency.

165 Arrangements for restoring supply should address procedures for repressurising those parts of the network which have been shut down, and the sequence in which supplies will be restored to consumers, taking into account priority consumer criteria and any consultation with the Department of Trade and Industry at that time. Particular arrangements for the reinstatement of supply to domestic consumers should be described, including checking all appliances for obvious visible signs of spillage of the products of combustion. These arrangements should take account of the speed at which reinstatement can be carried out safely. This is likely to be affected by the availability of sufficient competent personnel, safe working procedures, the need to follow procedures, including record keeping, and potential fatigue of personnel.

Interpretation

Schedule

1

22   *In this Schedule -*

    (a)   *"audit" means systematic assessment of the adequacy of the management system to achieve the purpose referred to in paragraph 6 carried out by persons who are sufficiently independent of the system (but who may be employed by the duty holder) to ensure that such assessment is objective;*

    (b)   *"management system" means the organisation and arrangements established by the duty holder for managing his undertaking;*

    (c)   *any reference to an operation intended to be undertaken by the duty holder is a reference to his intended operation of conveying gas in a network.*

166 Paragraph 22(a) and (b) of Schedule 1 defines the terms 'audit' and 'management system'. 'Management system' appears in paragraph 6 of Schedule 1 and in the definition of 'audit'. 'Audit' appears in paragraph 11 of Schedule 1.

167 Paragraph 22(c) of Schedule 1 makes clear that a safety case has to address all the matters listed in Schedules 1 to 3 in respect of the safe management of the flow of gas.

Particulars to be included in safety case of a network emergency co-ordinator

Regulation 3(2)

1   Name and address of the person preparing the safety case (in this Schedule referred to as "the duty holder").

2   A general description of the network to which the safety case relates, including the geographical location of where pipes used by different persons conveying gas in the network join.

168   The description of the network should cover only those characteristics which impinge on the safe management of gas flow. The aim is to provide sufficient background information about the structure of the network to enable HSE properly to assess the network emergency co-ordinator's (NEC's) safety case. This information should be presented in a logical manner and, as far as is possible, be self-supporting. Sufficient information, including where appropriate suitable plans or diagrams to show the length of various types of pipeline and the location of safety critical plant and equipment on the network, should be provided. This might include, for example, particulars of the interfaces between pipeline systems of different gas transporters, the location of terminal and storage facilities, control centres and the geographical areas covered by them. The names of relevant operators should also be included.

169   A general description of the operation of the network, sufficient to provide a proper understanding of the organisational arrangements for ensuring the overall safe management of the flow of gas in an actual or emerging supply emergency, should be provided. The information given should describe, in particular, the volumes of gas likely to be conveyed; the pressure and capacity constraints that exist; the circumstances where gas not conforming to the requirements of regulation 8(1) will be allowed in the network; the options available for rerouting gas through the network; and the means of communicating with, and collecting information from, each gas transporter on the network.

3   Particulars to demonstrate that the duty holder has established adequate arrangements for co-ordinating the actions to be taken to prevent a supply emergency including -

(a)   particulars to demonstrate that the duty holder has established adequate arrangements to monitor gas flow within the network in order to identify a forthcoming supply emergency;

170   The risk assessment carried out under paragraph 4 of Schedule 1 is likely to have identified a number of circumstances which could threaten the safe flow of gas in the network. These foreseeable events might include, for example, the threat of widespread industrial action, a significant failure in gas supply, catastrophic failure of a high pressure pipeline or a prolonged period of exceptionally cold weather. The measures necessary for dealing with such events form the basis of the information which should be included in the safety case.

171   As a first step, a clear definition of what constitutes a supply emergency needs to be established and described in the safety case. Supply emergencies tend to be of two types. First, there are those where there is sufficient gas available in the network, but a constraint on the network means that it is not physically possible to move the gas into the area where the emergency is

developing. Such circumstances generally give rise to local emergencies, the management of which rests with those gas transporters immediately affected (see paragraph 18 of Schedule 1). The second type of emergency, which will normally involve the NEC, is where there is insufficient gas to meet demand in a significant part of the network, and where there are not necessarily any physical constraints to prevent movement of the gas into the affected area, if it is, or could be made, available.

172 In periods of exceptionally cold weather, a network emergency may arise because the security of supply criteria are exceeded on any day or over a prolonged period. The safety case should set out the basis of the security of supply criteria.

173 In a network emergency the NEC would be responsible for co-ordinating actions across the affected parts of the network to minimise the possibility of a supply emergency developing; and where one develops, for minimising the safety consequences. This may mean giving directions to gas transporters about rerouting, reducing consumption on specific parts of the network, or for specific groups of consumers to cease using gas, and for ensuring that gas transporters have followed these directions. An example of a network supply emergency would be where a significant part of the network, such as two or more Local Distribution Zones (within the meaning of the BG TransCo Network Code) and any associated third party systems within these zones, were potentially or actually experiencing a supply emergency.

174 The safety case should provide details of the criteria to be used in each of the foreseeable events identified by the duty holder's risk assessment for declaring a network supply emergency. Account of the particular circumstances which might exist at any one time, including identification of the point, or points, at which the duty holder might need to exercise their override of control across all, or part of, the network, should be identified. Procedures for dealing with any further deterioration of the supply/demand imbalance will need to be described, in particular the decision to authorise the introduction of gas conforming to Part II of Schedule 3 into the network.

175 Effective monitoring of gas flow within the network will form an integral part of the duty holder's responsibilities. This will enable the NEC to take action to prevent, as far as possible, a supply emergency developing, and where it cannot be prevented, to take timely decisions in order to minimise the safety consequences. The safety case should set out the arrangements the duty holder has established for dealing with these circumstances, in particular the arrangements for obtaining sufficient relevant, timely and accurate information about the status of the supply, and the demand across the network. This might include information about, for example:

(a) the potential amount of gas which could be made available, including gas complying with Part II of Schedule 3;

(b) demand levels, location and status (firm or interruptible) of large consumers, ie above 25 000 therms per annum;

(c) where gas is being input and taken out of the network, pressure/capacity constraints and gas composition;

(d) consumption against anticipated demand during the day, eg due to adverse weather; and adjustments to planned input and associated lead times and actual performance;

(e) problems experienced by gas transporters, terminal and storage operators, and gas producers which could affect the delivery of gas flow commitments, eg plant failure, 'software' failures (computers, telecommunications); and

(f) routing/capacity constraints, eg planned maintenance.

176 The safety case should describe the contingency arrangements which would come into operation in the event of a communication or monitoring equipment failure.

(b) in cases where it is not possible to obtain sufficient gas, particulars of the procedures and arrangements that the duty holder has established to direct persons conveying gas to secure a reduction in consumption and to verify that such directions have been followed;

177 The particulars to be included in the safety case should cover both the means by which the supply emergency will be co-ordinated, and the procedures for securing any necessary reduction in gas consumption. The safety case should also set down the arrangements for informing all those with duties under these Regulations of their roles and responsibilities in a supply emergency.

178 These may need to include, for example, arrangements for operating an incident room, setting up and maintaining communications links with gas transporters, terminal and storage operators and shippers etc and ensuring the availability of sufficient competent personnel to manage the process effectively.

179 Details of the methods used for determining the allocation of available gas to gas transporters should be set down including, for example, the demand profile, actual consumption and ability of each part of the network to cut back consumption. The duty holder will need to take account of the risks to consumers, in particular domestic and other priority consumers, associated with the loss of supply of gas and subsequent reinstatement. This is likely to require a hierarchical approach to disconnection, which should take account of risks to different groups of consumers and any priority consumer criteria established by the Secretary of State for Trade and Industry. As far as possible the hierarchy should be based on objective engineering principles aimed at reducing to a minimum the safety risks arising from a supply emergency across the affected parts of the network. In practice, the duty holder and the gas transporters concerned will probably need to adopt a common approach across the network. The details of this should be recorded in gas transporters' safety cases, and that of the NEC.

180 The arrangements should also include details of the procedures for directing gas transporters to reduce consumption, the speed at which this should be achieved, and arrangements for individual gas transporters to confirm that action has been taken.

(c) particulars of the procedures that the duty holder has established to monitor the situation throughout a supply emergency, and details of the procedures established to restore safely the gas supply to consumers, once the emergency is over;

181 The safety case should describe the procedures established to monitor the status of gas flow and supply/demand across the network throughout a network supply emergency (see paragraph 175). The information collected as part of the monitoring process will need to be adequate to allow decisions to be made about whether further reductions in consumption are required, how long the supply emergency is likely to last, and when the end of the emergency can be declared on all, or parts, of the network affected by it.

182 To assist in the decision-making process, criteria should be developed for declaring an end to a supply emergency, and for bringing each affected part of the network back on stream. This may include considering the sequence in which supply should be reinstated to consumers, taking into account the circumstances of the emergency, the time of year, the ability of each gas transporter to effect reinstatement, and any consultations with the Department of Trade and Industry at that time. Details of the arrangements for ensuring gas transporters, shippers, terminal and storage operators etc are kept informed on the status of the emergency, and the action required of them, in particular the provision of information, should be included in the safety case.

183 There will also be a need to review the co-ordination and handling of a network supply emergency at the end of each emergency. This should be completed as soon as possible. The objective should be to identify the difficulties encountered, their causes, and where appropriate, for revised arrangements to be put in place. The review should examine detailed operational arrangements as well as the quality of the decision-making process. It will be necessary to ensure that lessons learnt, and revised arrangements, are communicated to all those concerned. Where appropriate amendments to the safety case should be made and if these constitute a material change, the duty holder's safety case should be resubmitted to HSE. There may also be a need for relevant gas transporters to resubmit their safety cases to HSE for acceptance.

(d) *particulars to demonstrate that the duty holder has established adequate arrangements to decide when and for how long gas not conforming with the requirements of regulation 8(1) should be conveyed in the network pursuant to regulation 8(2);*

184 Regulation 8(2) permits the duty holder to allow the introduction of gas which conforms to Part II of Schedule 3 where this is necessary to prevent a supply emergency. This provision exists because there may be circumstances in which the introduction of out-of-specification gas into the network is less undesirable in safety terms than the loss of supply, in particular to domestic and other small-volume consumers. The safety case should set out criteria for determining when this provision will be used, and the operational arrangements which have been established with gas transporters, probably through their respective Network Codes and associated operational protocols, for introducing and controlling the flow of gas conforming to Part II of Schedule 3 across the network.

(e) *particulars to demonstrate that the duty holder has established adequate arrangements for rehearsing and testing the actions to be taken in the case of a supply emergency;*

185 The safety case should describe arrangements for organising exercises to rehearse and test the actions which need to be taken in the event of a national supply emergency. The range of exercises carried out should be wide, including periodic full-scale exercises and more frequent testing of key components, eg communication with gas transporters. Exercises should be designed to involve the duty holder and other users of the network.

186 The safety case should also document arrangements made to inform HSE, in advance, of planned major exercises, so that HSE representatives can, where appropriate, arrange to observe.

187 Each exercise should be systematically reviewed by all those who participated in, or were affected by, it. Results of the review, including any necessary changes to procedures, should be communicated to gas transporters

and others, as appropriate. Safety cases should be updated, where necessary, and if appropriate, resubmitted to HSE.

(f)   a general description of the plant and premises the duty holder intends to use in connection with the arrangements and procedures described in his safety case pursuant to this paragraph.

188   A brief description should be given in the safety case of the facilities, plant and equipment used by the duty holder to discharge his duties. The information should be sufficient to support the arrangements and procedures set out in the safety case. This might include, for example, details of the communication and computer systems used, the facilities available to the duty holder to monitor gas flows etc, and the effective co-ordination of gas flow into and through the network. Particular attention should be paid to the arrangements made for back-up systems to come into play in the event of, for example, a computer or communications failure.

4   The same particulars as are referred to in paragraphs 4 to 11 of Schedule 1 as if any reference in paragraphs 4 and 6 thereof to the operation intended to be undertaken were a reference to the network emergency co-ordinator's functions under the arrangements and procedures described in his safety case.

189   The safety case should also include details of the arrangements made to comply with the requirements of paragraphs 4-11 of Schedule 1 as they apply to the NEC.

Content and other characteristics of gas

Regulation 8

Part I   Requirements under normal conditions

1   The content and characteristics of the gas shall be in accordance with the values specified in the following table.

Content or characteristic	Value
hydrogen sulphide content	$\leq 5\text{mg/m}^3$;
total sulphur content (including H_2S)	$\leq 50\text{mg/m}^3$;
hydrogen content	$\leq 0.1\%$ (molar);
oxygen content	$\leq 0.2\%$ (molar);
impurities	shall not contain solid or liquid material which may interfere with the integrity or operation of pipes or any gas appliance (within the meaning of regulation 2(1) of the 1994 Regulations) which a consumer could reasonably be expected to operate;
hydrocarbon dewpoint and water dewpoint	shall be at such levels that they do not interfere with the integrity or operation of pipes or any gas appliance (within the meaning of regulation 2(1) of the 1994 Regulations) which a consumer could reasonably be expected to operate;
WN	(i) ≤ 51.41 MJ/m^3, and
	(ii) ≥ 47.20 MJ/m^3;
ICF	≤ 0.48
SI	≤ 0.60

2   The gas shall have been treated with a suitable stenching agent to ensure that it has a distinctive and characteristic odour which shall remain distinctive and characteristic when the gas is mixed with gas which has not been so treated, except that this paragraph shall not apply where the gas is at a pressure of above 7 barg.

3   The gas shall be at a suitable pressure to ensure the safe operation of any gas appliance (within the meaning of regulation 2(1) of the 1994 Regulations) which a consumer could reasonably be expected to operate.

4   (1)   Expressions and abbreviations used in this Part shall have the meanings assigned to them in Part III of this Schedule.

      (2)   ICF and SI shall be calculated in accordance with Part III of this Schedule.

Part II   Requirements for gas conveyed to prevent a supply emergency

1   The requirements of the gas referred to in regulation 8(2) and (4) are -

   (a)   WN -

         (i) ≤ 52.85 MJ/m^3, and

         (ii) ≥ 46.50 MJ/m^3; and

   (b)   ICF ≤ 1.49,

and in all other respects the gas shall conform to the requirements specified in Part I of this Schedule, as if those requirements were repeated herein.

2   (1)   Expressions and abbreviations used in this Part shall have the meanings assigned to them in Part III of this Schedule.

    (2)   ICF and SI shall be calculated in accordance with Part III of this Schedule.

Part III   Interpretation

1   In this Schedule -

"bar" means bars (absolute);

"barg" means bars (guage);

"C" means degrees Celsius;

"C_3H_8" means the percentage by volume of propane in the equivalent mixture;

"equivalent mixture" means a mixture of methane, propane and nitrogen having the same characteristics as the gas being conveyed and calculated as follows -

    (i)   the hydrocarbons in the gas being conveyed, other than methane and propane, are expressed as an equivalent amount of methane and propane which has the same ideal volume and the same average number of carbon atoms per molecule as the said hydrocarbons, and

    (ii)   the equivalents derived from (i) above, together with an equivalent for all of the inert gases in the gas being conveyed, expressed as nitrogen, are normalised to 100%, such that the equivalent mixture of methane, propane and nitrogen has a Wobbe Number equal to that of the gas being conveyed;

"ICF" means the Incomplete Combustion Factor;

"mg/m^3" means milligrams per cubic metre at 15C and 1.01325 bar;

"MJ/m^3" means megajoules per cubic metre where the calorific value of a dry gas is determined on the basis that the water produced by combustion is assumed to be condensed;

"N_2" means the percentage by volume of nitrogen in the equivalent mixture;

"PN" means the sum of the percentages by volume of propane and nitrogen in the equivalent mixture;

"relative density" means the ratio of the mass of a volume of the gas when containing no water vapour to the mass (expressed in the same units) of the same volume of air containing no water vapour under the same conditions of temperature and pressure;

"SI" means the Soot Index;

"WN" means the Wobbe Number;

trigonometric functions are to be evaluated in radians.

190 The Wobbe Number of gases should be determined on the basis that any water vapour in the gas has first been removed.

2 In this Schedule, ICF, SI and WN shall be calculated in accordance with the following formulae -

$$ICF = \frac{WN-50.73+0.03PN}{1.56}$$

$$SI = 0.896 \tan^{-1}(0.0255C_3H_8 - 0.0233N_2 + 0.617)$$

$$WN = \frac{\text{calorific value}}{\sqrt{\text{relative density}}}$$

Guidance on determining whether gases fall within the criteria set out in Parts I and II of Schedule 3

191 The characteristics of a gas which can be accepted into the network under normal conditions (Part I of this Schedule), and those which may be authorised by the NEC (Part II of this Schedule) to prevent a supply emergency, have been derived from work carried out by Dutton et al (see references on page 51) on gas interchangeability. The work was carried out against a background of declining gas supplies from the southern North Sea and replacement supplies being provided from an increasing number of other sources. It was necessary to ensure that these new gas supplies were interchangeable with existing supplies, and that established standards of appliance performance and safety could be maintained without the need to adjust appliances.

192 Gases from diverse sources were burned on several types of gas appliance and their performance observed. From this parameters were established within which gases could be safely consumed. This led to the production of a 3-dimensional diagram together with equations for calculating the related indices for gases that contained significant quantities of hydrogen, and a simplified 2-dimensional version of the diagram for essentially hydrogen-free gases. As gases supplied to the UK are hydrogen-free, the 2-dimensional diagram, modified to suit existing conditions, has been used. The diagram has axes of Wobbe Number and equivalent mixture (propane plus nitrogen).

193 The following technique should be used to determine whether a particular gas composition complies with these Regulations:

(a) The Wobbe Number (real, gross) is calculated by methods outlined in International Standard ISO 6976: *Natural gas - calculation of calorific values, density, relative density and Wobbe index from composition* 2nd Edition 1995, at standard conditions of 15C and 1.01325 bar.

(b) The equivalent composition of the gas (and hence the equivalent propane plus nitrogen) is calculated as follows:

    (i) the non-methane/propane hydrocarbons are converted to methane and propane in accordance with Dutton, where:

        • all isomeric forms of an alkane (eg, normal, iso and neo pentane) have the same equivalence;

        • alkenes and aromatic components have the same equivalence as the alkane of the same carbon number;

48

(ii) all the inert gases are expressed as an amount of nitrogen which when added to the amounts of methane and propane from (i) above, and normalised to 100%, gives a mixture having the same Wobbe Number (real, gross) as the original gas.

The normalised mixture in (ii) is also the equivalent gas having the equivalent amounts of propane plus nitrogen.

(c) Acceptable gas mixtures are those where the intersection of Wobbe Number and equivalent mixture (propane plus nitrogen) lies within the envelope of gas conforming to Parts I or II of this Schedule depending on the circumstances.

Worked example for calculating equivalent mixtures

Normalised gas composition (molar%)

Methane	93.17
Ethane	3.26
Propane	0.67
Isobutane	0.27
Isopentane	0.08
Hexanes	0.05
Heptanes	0.03
Octanes	0.01
Carbon dioxide	0.34
Nitrogen	2.12
Total	100.00

(a) From ISO 6976 this gives:

Calorific value (gross)	38.62077 MJ/m^3
Relative density	0.5971955
Wobbe Number (gross)	49.97622 MJ/m^3

(b) (i) From Dutton: conversion of hydrocarbons to methane and propane

		Methane	*Propane*
Methane	93.170	93.170	0.000
Ethane	3.260	1.630	1.630
Propane	0.670	0.000	0.670
Isobutane	0.270	−0.135	0.405
Isopentane	0.080	−0.080	0.160
Hexanes	0.050	−0.075	0.125
Heptanes	0.030	−0.060	0.090
Octanes	0.010	−0.025	0.035
Total	97.540	94.425	3.115

Calculating equivalent nitrogen and equivalent mixture:

$$WN_{(real)} = \frac{CV_{real}}{\sqrt{SG_{real}}}$$

Using the terms in ISO 6976:

$$WN_{(real)} = \frac{H_{real}}{\sqrt{d_{real}}} = \frac{H_{ideal}/Z_{mix}}{\sqrt{d_{ideal} \times \dfrac{Z_{air}}{Z_{mix}}}}$$

$$WN^2{}_{real} = \frac{H^2{}_{ideal}/Z^2{}_{mix}}{d_{ideal} \times \dfrac{Z_{air}}{Z_{mix}}} = \frac{H^2{}_{ideal}}{d_{ideal} \times Z_{air} \times Z_{mix}}$$

or $\quad WN^2{}_{real} \times d_{ideal} \times Z_{air} \times Z_{mix} = H^2{}_{ideal} \qquad \qquad \ldots(1)$

(b) (ii) For the three component mixtures of:

	Moles
Methane	0.94425
Propane	0.03115
Nitrogen	X
Total	0.9754+X

and using values in ISO 6976:

$$d_{ideal} = \frac{0.94425 \times 0.5539}{(0.9753+X)} + \frac{0.3115 \times 1.5225}{(0.9754+X)} + \frac{0.9672X}{(0.9754+X)}$$

$$= \frac{0.5704460 + 0.9672X}{(0.9754+X)}$$

$$Z_{mix} = 1 - \left[\frac{0.94425 \times 0.0447}{(0.9754+X)} + \frac{0.03115 \times 0.1338}{(0.9754+X)} + \frac{0.0173X}{(0.9754+X)} \right]^2$$

$$= 1 - \left[\frac{0.0463758 + 0.0173X}{(0.9754+X)} \right]^2$$

$$H_{ideal} = \frac{0.94425 \times 37.706}{(0.9754+X)} + \frac{0.03115 \times 93.94}{(0.9754+X)} = \frac{38.530122}{(0.9754+X)}$$

$$WN = 49.97622$$

$$Z_{air} = 0.99958$$

50

Substituting into (1) and calculating out gives:

$$X^3 + 2.5395701X^2 + 1.4845081X - 0.039834584 = 0$$

Solving for X gives 0.0256928

Thus:

	Moles	*Equivalent mixture (%)*
Methane	0.9442500	94.32193
Propane	0.0311500	3.11160
Nitrogen	0.0256928	2.56647
Total	1.0010928	100.00000

(c) Find intersection (1) of equivalent mixture and Wobbe Number on the gas interchangeability diagram (Figure 2).

References

1 Dutton B C, 'A new dimension to gas interchangeability', Communication 1246, 50th Autumn Meeting at Eastbourne, Institution of Gas Engineers, 1984

2 Dutton B C and Gimzewski E, 'Gas interchangeability: prediction of flame lift' *Journal of the Institute of Energy*, June 1983, p107

3 Dutton B C and Wood S W, 'Gas interchangeability: prediction of soot deposition on domestic gas appliances with aerated burners', *Journal of the Institute of Energy*, September 1984, p381

4 Dutton B C and Souchard R J, 'Gas interchangeability: prediction of incomplete combustion', *Journal of the Institute of Energy*, December 1985, p210

Printed and published by the Health and Safety Executive

Figure 2   Gas interchangeability diagram

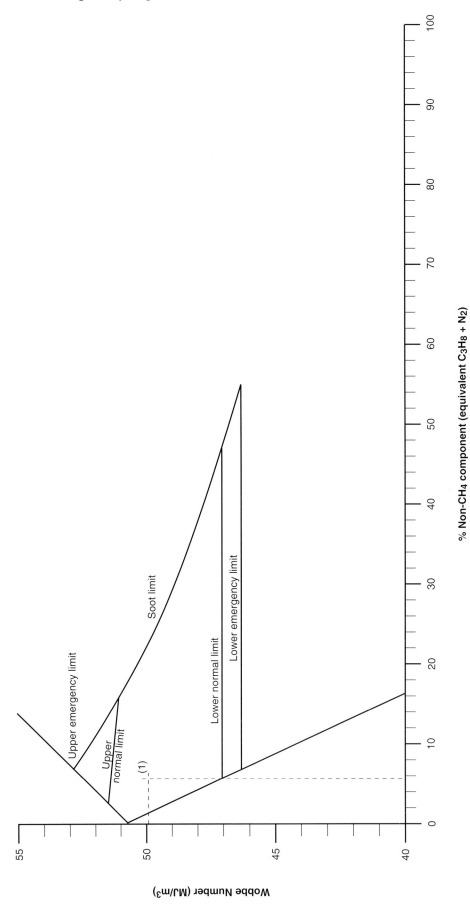